2 0₽

DEAR WORRIED BROWN EYES

DEAR WORRIED BROWN EYES

ROSEMARY RATCLIFF

ROBERT MAXWELL : PUBLISHER
LONDON

Pergamon Press Ltd., Headington Hill Hall, Oxford
4 & 5 Fitzroy Square, London W.1
Pergamon Press (Scotland) Ltd., 2 & 3 Teviot Place, Edinburgh 1
Pergamon Press Inc., Maxwell House, Fairview Park, Elmsford,
New York 10523
Pergamon of Canada Ltd., 207 Queen's Quay West, Toronto 1
Pergamon Press (Aust.) Pty. Ltd., 19a Boundary Street, Rushcutters Bay,
N.S.W. 2011, Australia
Pergamon Press S.A.R.L., 24 rue des Écoles, Paris 5°
Vieweg & Sohn GmbH, Burgplatz 1, Braunschweig

First edition 1969

Reprinted 1969

Library of Congress Catalog Card No. 68–59083

Printed in Great Britain by A. Wheaton & Co., Exeter

08 007041 8

Acknowledgements

My thanks are due to all the unknown people whose problems provided material for the book – and also to their patient advisors, known or unknown.

Acknowledgements are due to the following:

Fleetway Publications Ltd.
Home Companion, Family Journal & Weekly Friend, Home Mirror, Lucky Charm, Mirabelle, Woman's Weekly

Fleetway Publications Ltd. and Marjorie Proops
Woman's Mirror, Woman's Sunday Mirror

Fleetway Publications Ltd. and Clare Shepherd
Woman's Realm

George Newnes Ltd.
Betty's Weekly, Lady's Companion, Peg's Paper, Woman's Friend, Woman's Sphere

George Newnes Ltd. and Mary Grant
Woman's Own

Odhams Press Ltd. and Evelyn Home
Woman

Associated Newspapers Ltd.
Daily Mail and *Weekend*

Cassell & Company Ltd.
The Penny Magazine

My thanks are also due to *Punch* for permission to use the drawing on the cover.

Foreword

You're seventeen and have just quarrelled with your boy friend. It seems like the end of the world. You don't like to ask your mother for help because somehow you and she don't speak the same language any more. So you pour out your troubles to a complete stranger instead.

Not that the person receiving the woes seems so remote. Her words of sympathy and advice will have appeared weekly or monthly in a favourite women's magazine. She will have become a super 'aunt' figure, all knowing, all understanding.

The letter joins several hundred others on her desk, some frivolous, some serious. From girls contemplating suicide, to girls worried about spots, they all have one thing in common – they've reached the point where they need outside help.

The mothers who smile at their daughters' boy friends are not so invulnerable, either. Despite doctors and Marriage Guidance Councillors, they still find it easier to confide marital problems on to paper. Even men swallow their pride and write in.

Hundreds of problems a week are dealt with by this system of remote control; it's impossible to judge with what degree of success. Perhaps merely putting pen to paper helps some people. Perhaps the Aunt Aggies persuade the more serious cases to seek expert, first-hand help. Whatever the outcome, it's a thought-provoking reflection that however sophisticated society appears to be, we still carry such a burden of personal problems without the apparatus to solve them on the spot.

The frailty of our personal lives becomes even more poignant when you consider another scene. This time the woman is in her late twenties or early thirties. She longs to get married, but feels all her chances have passed her by. 'Where,' she writes pathetically to the most popular answers column, 'can I find a husband?' The date – 1691.

Some problems in the 270 year span of this collection are universal. Some are so particular to their time they can raise nothing but an incredulous giggle. Even allowing for the oppressive atmosphere of Victorian England, did girls seriously worry about wearing coloured stockings on a bicycle or sharing an umbrella with a young male acquaintance? But the answers are deadly serious —both moves are considered most improper.

The magazines throw up both major and minor social movements in sharp relief. When the French Revolution preached Liberty, Fraternity, Equality, some English misses took the slogan into the drawing room and began whooping it up in a very contemporary manner. Clothes became masculine, virginity was decried and the older generation reduced to crying helplessly, 'Where will it all end?'

Well, it ended with the Victorian Age and here, too, the letters show up variations within those clammy, claustrophobic sixty-odd years. Mothers ask about beating their daughters and reveal the sexual thrill they got from a piece of sadism that is justified, oh so nicely, by the prevailing code of moral education. A woman has been recommended alcohol as a stimulant by her doctor, and is now hooked on the bottle. There was a flourishing trade in marriage market magazines, with all classes advertising the hopeful details of their desirability – an Aunt Aggie advises a reader *not* to use the medium.

The gradual metamorphosis of emancipated woman is neatly chartered. In 1865 a woman is ticked off for making friends with a woman beneath her own position. By 1902 a girl who is worried about marrying a man 'in a lower position socially' is told that love will conquer all. In 1905 magazines have to face the problem of working girls living alone in lodgings; by 1906 girls are going off on group holidays with their boy friends. By 1907 the modern era has really arrived when a typist complains about the unwelcome attentions of the boss's son.

Sexual emancipation starts in the 1930's with the first queries about sleeping with boy friends. Aunt Aggies, as bastions of the nation's morals, may have followed every liberalising trend so far, but here they hold fast. Apart from a Marjorie Proops letter which suggests the best treatment for a wayward daughter is to give her contraceptive advice, the answer is always 'no' to sex before marriage.

Will the Pill force the Aunt Aggies into another, radical change of attitude? Will men, now outnumbered by girls, eventually become the sex with the love problems? Will Aunt Aggies become a dominating influence as home and church power ebbs? There is one thing for sure. Just as comedy acts as an outlet for our feelings of insecurity, so problem pages help us face our own infallibility. No personal relationship is ever without its problems; it is comforting to be reminded week after week just how difficult it is to be a human being.

1691–1720

IN 1690 a London bookseller called John Dunton had a brilliant and apparently original idea – that human beings themselves could make more interesting newspaper material than affairs of state. His twice-weekly publication, *The Athenian Mercury*, aroused interest very simply by using nothing but readers' problems. In the various sections, 'Science', 'Metaphysical', 'Love', readers queried and Dunton's team of experts answered.

The people who wrote in to *The Athenian Mercury* were mainly of a class that was fast disappearing – semi-rural, self-supporting families where the husband was probably a craftsman or small tradesmen, the wife a skilled practitioner in all household crafts. Running a home and business was a partnership, abrasive sometimes, but genuine.

At the end of the seventeenth century agricultural and cottage industries gave way to more sophisticated, town-based manufacturing. As families had more money and more servants, women lost their household rôle and became ornaments or status symbols for their husbands. Feminine idleness was a sign of gentility.

Without a common interest, men and women became more artificial and mannered towards each other, and the elaborate, rumbustious Restoration style of courtship spread down through society. John Evelyn mourned at the turn of the century the days when men 'chose their wives for their modesty, frugality, keeping at home, good housewifery'. But in the battle between prudery and licentiousness that marks English life, the latter was on the ascendent.

Gentlemen, I'm a tradesman, and live in reasonable good credit amongst my neighbours; I follow my business, and by my labour, together with God's blessing, I procure a competent maintenance for my family. My common expense doth not exceed 3d a day, except occasioned by a relation or some other person, for or in whom I have either esteem or interest, and yet I am under the misfortune of having a wife that will often upbraid me with drunkenness and idleness, both of which I am utterly averse to. Now I desire to know whether, after all other methods used in vain, I may not make use of stripes in order to the bringing of her to a more prudent behaviour. I look upon't as matter of conscience, and therefore desire your speedy answer, which if you grant, you will infinitely oblige your very humble servant.

Stripes! No, sir, by no means, unless you have a mind to fall under the Woman's Surgery. Get a pretty little padlock for her tongue, and then it will be troublesome to move it without disobliging the inhabitants of her mouth; or if that won't do, draw a tooth once a day, or after every lecture; or lastly, procure a preferment for her in Bedlam, and then you may promise yourself a little quiet.

ATHENIAN MERCURY, JULY 7TH, 1691

Where is the likeliest place to get a Husband in?

Poor distressed lady! Had we but her Name we should go near to insert an Advertisement for her at end of our *Mercury*: But since she had left us in the dark, she must e'en be content with the best directions we can give her in this weighty matter. We answer then, that 'tis the likeliest place to get a lover where there are fewest Women: and accordingly, if she will venture to ship herself for some Plantations by the next Fleet, if she is but anything marketable, she is bound to win but one or other.

Whether it is lawful to marry a person one cannot love, only in compliance to relations and to get an estate?

Had the question only been proposed of such as we don't actually love it might perhaps have admitted of some limitation, since we sometimes see persons love tenderly after marriage, who could hardly endure each other's sight before. . . . But as 'tis proposed here 'tis beyond all doubt, and must be answered in the negative, since such a practice would be both the most cruel and imprudent thing in the world.

Whether the woman's condition in marriage be not worse than the man's?

That's much as she manages it. Nature has generally given the fair sex art enough by which if either she herself, or custom, or law has given ours any advantage they may if they please recover more than their own again. In childbirth only they have without doubt much the heavier part of the load; and then they have much more reason to wish the world might propagate like trees. . . .

When we are in Love, and the man won't or can't understand our Signs and Omens; what in Modesty can we do more to Open their eyes?

Alas poor lady! Your case is very hard. Why, pull 'em by the nose, write to 'em; or if neither of these will do (as you have been formerly advised) show 'em this Question and Answer in *The Athenian Mercury.*

Why love generally turns to coldness and neglect after marriage?

One great cause we believe to be the custom of the age. We have seen some kings' reigns, wherein it has been thought an abominable scandal for a man to love his own wife. If things had gone on, nothing would have been thought a greater disgrace than to have been born in wedlock. But to be ingenious, there seems to be something deeper in the case. Satiety commonly breeds loathing, and even manna every day would make one weary on it. But this variety may be obtained, this satiety may be cured, where there is a virtuous love, grounded on sympathy, and discretion hides those faults which are generally discovered after marriage, or by degrees removes them. If not, virtuous love excuses or at least balances them, and wit has always something entertaining and new which keeps the sweets of matrimony from growing rapid, dull and disagreeable.

Whether it be really a Happiness to have a handsome wife?

An happiness we think it is to have a fine woman; but as the lewd world goes, we must own a very dangerous happiness.

Who are wisest, those that marry for love, or for convenience?

There is no degree of wisdom in either. Love without the necessary conveniences of life will soon wear threadbare and conveniences without love is no better than being chained to a post for the sake of a little meat, drink and clothing. But if we compare the two, much love and moderate conveniency is far better than the most plentiful estate with little or no love.

Sir, You seem in many of your Writings to be a Man of a very compassionate Temper, and well acquainted with the Passion of Love. This encourages me to apply meself to you in my present Distress, which I believe you will look upon to be very great, and treat with Tenderness, notwithstanding it wholly arises from Love, and that it is a Woman that makes this Confession. I am now in the Twenty third Year of my Age, and have for a great while entertained the Adresses of a Man, who I thought loved me more than Life. I am sure I did him; and must own to you, not without some Confusion, That I have thought on nothing else for these Two long Years, but the happy Life we should lead together, and Means I should use to make myself still dearer to him. My fortune was indeed much beyond his, and as I was always in the Company of my Relations, he was forced to discover his Inclinations, and declare himself to me by Stories of other Persons, kind Looks, and many Ways which he knew too well that I understood. Oh! Mr. Bickerstaff, it is impossible to tell you how industrious I have been to make him appear lovely in my Thoughts. I made it a Point of Conscience to think well of him, and of no Man else. But he has since had an Estate fallen to him, and makes Love to another of a greater Fortune than mine. I could not believe the Report of this at first; but about a Fortnight ago I was convinced of the Truth of it by his own Behaviour. He came to give our Family a formal Visit, when, as there were several in Company, and many Things talked of, the Discourse fell upon some unhappy Woman who was in my own Circumstances. It was said by one in the Room, That they could not believe the Story could be true, because they did not believe any Man could be so false. Upon which, I stole a Look upon him with an Anguish not to be expressed. He saw my Eyes full of Tears; yet had the Cruelty to say, That he could see no Falsehood in Alterations of this Nature, where there had been no Contracts or Vows interchanged. Pray, do not make a Jest of Misery, but tell me seriously your Opinion of his Behaviour, and if you can have any Pity for my Condition, publish this in your next Paper, that being the only Way I have of complaining of his Unkindness and showing him the Injustice he has done me.

I am

Your humble Servant,

The unfortunate Statira.

The Name my Correspondent gives herself, puts me in Mind of my old Reading in Romances, and brings into my Thoughts a Speech of the Renowned Don Bellianis, who, upon a Complaint made him of a discourteous Knight that had left his injured Paramour in the same Manner, dries up her Tears with a Promise of Relief. 'Desconsolate Damsel, (quoth he) a foul Disgrace it were to all right worthy Professors of Chivalry, if such a Blot to Knighthood should pass unchastised. Give me to know the Abode of this recreant Lover, and I will give him as a Feast to the Fowls of the Air, or drag him bound before you at my Horse's Tail.'

I am not ashamed to own myself a Champion of distressed Damsels, and would venture as far to relieve them as Don Bellianis; for which Reason, I do invite this Lady to let me know the Name of the Traitor who has deceived her, and do promise not only her, but all the Fair Ones of Great Britain who lie under the same Calamity, to employ my Right Hand for their Redress, and serve them to my last Drop of Ink.

7

A lady hath obliged me to choose a husband for her, and if the question don't puzzle Apollo, I desire to know by what infallible mark I may find a good humoured man, but if I inquire for what is not in nature, then one that will make a civil husband?

Let him be of a suitable age and condition; of an even temper, and stranger to the spleen; learned, without pedantry; well bred, without affectation; abounding more in sense than wit; well travelled thro' himself; the consciousness of his own ignorance will restrain him from a contempt of his wife; fully acquainted with the town, without being touched by the vices of it; slow of promise, but sudden of performance; as apt to take as to give an affront; tender and compassionate, but firm to his honour. To all this let there be added a good estate, the want of which sometimes sours the best dispositions. Now, to acquaint you where to meet with such a person. . . . But that is without the limits of your question.

THE BRITISH APOLLO (BETWEEN 1707 AND 1711)

Gentlemen, I am an old maid as times go now, but have an inclination after a young man — nay, in short, a desire to wed; but I am pretty sensible that there is nothing more despicable than a gray virgin, which makes me fear he hath not such a strong desire after me as I have for him, but I have as much gold as will balance my years; but there is a wretched old bachelor in the way, almost as old as myself, pretends a zealous affection for me or my money. I leave you to be my judge.

Indeed, Miss Abigail, your case requires haste, since you are gray already. We will not detain you any longer than to advise you, which either comes first, turn the lock, snatch out the key, and let your maid whip out of the window for a parson to secure him, lest your staying for a second thought loses both.

8

Sir, you cannot think it strange if I, who know little of the world, apply to you for advice in the weighty affair of matrimony, since you yourself have often declared it to be of that consequence as to require the utmost deliberation. Without further preface therefore, give me leave to tell you, that my father at his death left me a fortune sufficient to make me a match for any gentleman. My mother (for she is still alive) is very pressing with me to marry; and I am apt to think, to gratify her, I shall venture upon one of two gentlemen who at this time make their addresses to me. My request is, that you would direct me in my choice; which that you may the better do, I shall give you their characters; and to avoid confusion, desire you to call them by the names of Philander and Silvius. Philander is young and has a good estate; Silvius is as young, and has a better. The former has had a liberal education, has seen the town, is retired from thence to his estate in the country, is a man of few words and much given to books. The latter was brought up under his father's eye, who gave him just learning enough to keep his accounts; but made withal very expert in country business, such as ploughing, sowing, buying, selling, and the like. They are both very sober men, neither of their persons is disagreeable, nor did I know which to prefer till I had heard them discourse; when the conversation of Philander so much prevailed, as to give him the advantage with me in all other respects. My mother pleads strongly for Silvius; and uses these arguments, that he not only has the larger estate at present, but by his good husbandry and management increases it daily; that his little knowledge in other affairs will make him easy and tractable; wheras (according to her) men of letters know too much to make good husbands. To part of this I imagine I answer effectually, by saying, Philander's estate is large enough; that they who think £2000 a year sufficient make no difference between that and three. I easily believe him less conversant in those affairs, the knowledge of which she so much commends in Silvius; but I think them neither so necessary or becoming in a gentleman, as the accomplishments of Philander. It is no great character of a man to say, he rides in his coach and six and understands as much as he who follows the plough. Add to this, that the conversation *of these sort of men seems so disagreeable to me, that though they make good bailiffs, I can hardly be persuaded they can be good companions. Tis possible I may seem to have odd notions, when I say I am not fond of a man only for being of (what is called) a thriving temper. To conclude, I own I am at a loss to conceive how good sense should make a man an ill husband, or conversing with books less complaisant.* Caelia.

The resolution which this lady is going to take, she may very well say is founded on reason: for after the necessities of life are served, there is no manner of competition between a man of a liberal education and illiterate. Men are not altered by their circumstances, but as they give them opportunities of exerting what they are in themselves; and a powerful clown is a tyrant in the most ugly form he can possibly appear. There lies a seeming objection in the thoughtful manner of Philander; but let her consider which she shall oftner have occasion to wish, that Philander would speak, or Silvius hold his tongue.

THE BRITISH APOLLO (BETWEEN 1707 AND 1711)

Gentlemen, I have long admired a young lady that sits over against me at church, to whom I have sent several letters, none of which are answered otherwise than to forbid me ever looking at her. Now, I believe they are read and answered by some other person, since I never see her, but she seems to love me as much as I her, our eyes being seldom off each other; and if I endeavour to obey her (supposed) letter, which is, not to look at her, she sits seemingly displeased with me, till my eyes are on her again. Now, Gentlemen, what shall I do in this case, since I cannot possibly come to the speech of her?

Repent that you spent your time so ill at church, and then, if your designs are just and honourable, you may have better hopes that heaven will prosper them.

I have lived a pure and undefiled virgin these 27 years; and I assure you, 'tis with great grief and sorrow of heart I tell you, that I become weary and impatient of the derision of the gigglers of our sex, who call me old maid and tell me I shall lead apes. If you are truly a patron of the distressed and an adept in astrology, you will advise whether I shall or ought to be prevailed upon by the impertinences of my own sex, to give way to the importunities of yours.

I must defer my answer to this lady out of a point of chronology. She says, she has been 27 years a maid; but I fear, according to a common error, she dates her virginity from her birth, which is a very erroneous method; for a woman of 20 is no more to be thought chaste so many years, than a man of that age can be said to have been so long valiant. We must not allow people the favour of a virtue till they have been under the temptation to the contrary. Woman is not a maid till her birthday, as we call it, of her fifteenth year. My plaintiff is therefore desired to inform me, whether she is at present in her 28th or 43rd year, and she shall be dispatched accordingly.

Sir, I have a great mind to be rid of my wife, and hope, when you consider my case, you will be of opinion I have very just pretensions to a divorce ... you are to know, Mr Spectator, that there are women who do not let their husbands see their faces till they are married. Not to keep you in suspense, I mean plainly, that part of the sex who paint. They are some of them so exquisitely skilful this way, that give them but a tolerable pair of eyes to set up with, and they will make bosom, lips, cheeks, and eyebrows by their own industry. As for my dear, never man was so inamour'd as I was of her fair forehead, neck and arms, as well as the bright jet of her hair; but to my great astonishment, I find they were all the effect of art. Her skin is so tarnished with this practice, that when she first wakes in a morning she scarce seems young enough to be the mother of her whom I carried to bed the night before. I shall take the liberty to part with her by the first opportunity, unless her father will make her portion suitable to her real, not her assumed countenance.

I cannot tell what the law or the parents of the lady will do for this injured gentleman, but must allow he hast very much justice on his side. I have indeed very long observed this evil and distinguished those of our women who wear their own, from those in borrowed complexions, by the *Picts* and the *British*. . . . The British have a lively, animated aspect; the Picts, though never so beautiful, have dead uninformed countenances. . . . A Pict, although she takes all that pains to invite the approach of lovers, is obliged to keep them at a certain distance; a sigh in a languishing lover, if fetched too near her, would dissolve a feature; and a kiss, snatched by a forward one, might transfer the complexion of the mistress to the admirer. . . .

THE SPECTATOR, DECEMBER 21ST, 1711

. . . I happened some days past to be at the play, where, during the time of performance, I could not keep my eyes off from a beautiful young creature who sat just before me and who I have been since informed has no fortune. It would utterly ruin my reputation for discretion to marry such a one, and by what I can learn she has a character of great modesty, so that there is nothing to be thought on any other way. My mind has ever since been so wholly bent on her that I am much in danger of doing something very extravagant without your speedy advice.

I am sorry I cannot answer this impatient gentleman but by another question. 'Would you marry to please other people or yourself?'

My eldest daughter, a girl of sixteen, has for some time been under the tuition of Monsieur Rigadoon, a Dancing-Master in the City; and I was prevailed upon by her and her mother to go last night to one of his balls. . . . I must acquaint you that very great abuses are crept into this entertainment. I was amazed to see my girl handed by, and handing young fellows with so much familiarity; and I could not have thought it had been in the child. They very often made use of a most impudent and lascivious step called 'Setting', which I know not how to describe to you, but by telling you that 'tis the very reverse of 'Back to Back'. At last an impudent young dog bid the fiddlers to play a dance called Mol Pately, and after having made two or three capers, ran to his partner, locked his arms in hers, and whisked her round cleverly above ground in such manner, that I, who sat upon one of the lowest benches, saw further above her shoe than I think fit to acquaint you with.

I must confess I am afraid that my correspondent had too much reason to be a little out of humour at the treatment of his daughter, but I conclude that he might have been much more so had he seen one of those kissing dances, in which, Will Honeycomb assures me, they are obliged to dwell almost a minute on the fair one's lips or they will be too quick for the music and dance quite out of time. I am not able, however, to give my final sentence against this diversion . . . so much of dancing, at least, as belongs to the behaviour and a handsome carriage of the body is extremely useful, if not absolutely necessary. . . .

I keep a coffee-house. . . . What I ask of you, is, to acquaint my customers (who are otherwise very good ones) that I am unavoidably hasped in my bar and cannot help hearing the improper discourses they are pleased to entertain me with. They strive who shall say the most immodest things in my hearing. At the same time half a dozen of them loll at the bar staring just in my face, ready to interpret my looks and gestures according to their own imaginations. In this passive condition I know not where to cast my eyes, place my hands, or what to employ myself in. But this confusion is to be a jest, and I hear them say in the end, with an insipid air of mirth and subtlety, 'Let her alone, she knows as well as we, for all she looks so.' Good Mr Spectator, persuade Gentlemen that it is out of all decency. Say it is possible a woman may be modest, and yet keep a public house. . . . I do assure you, sir, the cheerfulness of life which would arise from the honest gain I have, is utterly lost to me, from the endless, flat, impertinent pleasantries which I hear from morning to night. . . .

. . . This correspondent is not the only sufferer in this kind, for I have long letters both from the Royal and New-Exchange on the same subject. They tell me that a young fop cannot buy a pair of gloves but he is at the same time straining for some ingenious ribaldry to say to the young woman who helps them on. . . . If one might be serious on this prevailing folly, one might observe that it is a melancholy thing when the world is mercenary even to the buying and selling our very persons, that young women, though they have never so great attractions from nature, are never the nearer being happily disposed of in marriage. It is very hard under this necessity it shall not be possible for them to go into a way of trade for their maintenance, but their very excellencies and personal perfections shall be a disadvantage to them, and subject them to be treated as if they stood there to sell their persons to prostitution. . . . A woman is naturally more helpless than the other sex and a man of honour and sense should have this in his view in all manner of commerce with her. . . .

I have a couple of nieces under my direction who so often run gadding abroad, that I don't know where to have them. Their dress, their tea and their visits take up all their time and they go to bed as tired with doing nothing as I am after quilting a whole under-petticoat. . . . The only time they are not idle is while they read your Spectators; which being dedicated to the interests of virtue, I desire you to recommend the long neglected art of needle-work. Those hours which in the age are thrown away in dress, play, visits and the like were employed in my time in writing our recipes or working beds, chairs and hangings for the family. . . . It grieves my heart to see a couple of proud idle flirts sipping their tea for a whole afternoon in a room hung round with the industry of their great-grandmother. . . .

. . . This is, methinks, the most proper way wherein a lady can show a fine genius and I cannot forbear wishing that several writers of that sex had chosen to apply themselves rather to tapestry than rhyme. . . . Another argument for busying good women in works of fancy is because it takes them off from scandal. . . . While they are forming their birds and beasts, their neighbours will be allowed to be the fathers of their own children; and whig and tory will be but seldom mentioned where the great dispute is, whether blue or red is the more proper colour. . . .

1720–1815

DURING the eighteenth century 'genial coarseness' between the sexes gradually refined into a more gentle sensibility. Then revolutionary ideas from France filtered through into women's cosy world and in 1792 the whole country rocked to Mary Wollstonecraft's *Vindication of the Rights of Women* which suggested that higher education for women might lead them into careers and so into independence.

War with France set moral values spinning once again. Reinforced with ideas of equality, women were hell bent on emancipation, at least in the immediate social field. Their clothes became provocatively revealing and courtship was once more a lusty affair.

'It is quite a mistaken notion to think,' said one enlightened female, 'that it is our duty on all occasions to thwart our inclinations, and oppose the bent of our passions. This were as absurd as to think to prevent a river from flowing by stemming its currents.' Another writes in to a magazine and refers to virginity as 'a state too unnatural for any woman to be happy in.'

The older generation reacted predictably. 'I wish you could induce your fair readers to consider whether the ease of modern days is a good substitute for that dignity which formerly marked the gentlewoman, and whether the depravity of morals may not be traced to the laxity of morals, which in proscribing form and introducing familiarities has smoothed the way to impropriety.'

I am a Lady of Figure in this Country, and have a long Time convers'd, and kept Company with a Gentleman of a good Estate, who often visits the Family where I live, in all which Time I have never fail'd (as far as Modesty would allow me) to give him such evident Proofs, and made such fair Advances (which he himself if not altogether blind can justify) as become a Person so much his superior in Rank and Dignity, to assure him of my Passion; and yet I find I have no Reason to hope for good Success from all my Endeavours, tho' as nicely in as a Woman of my Experience cou'd be thought to do. I must therefore beg the Favour, as you have shewn yourself a Friend to our Sex, that you will give this Letter a Place in your next Journal, together with your Advice, how I shall manage henceforward with Safety to my Character, in Order to gain my so much wish'd for End. I shall impatiently wait for what is so heartily desir'd by

Your humble Servant, R.A.S.

The best and most immediate Advice I can give my fair Correspondent, is to shew the Gentleman this Paper herself, which perhaps may be a Means to awake him from his Lethargy. If not, and that she finds her Passion still grow upon her, let her impose a Restraint hereafter on her open and unreserv'd Behaviour, wherewith she has hitherto undeservedly entertain'd him; for some Men are soonest gain'd that Way, and like true Spaniels increase their Esteem by the Severity of their Usuage; and if that fails, let her write to him after such an anonymous Manner, that he may suspect her for the Author. But if all won't do, my humble Opinion is that the unfortunate Spark is either preingag'd to some other, and will not open his Eyes, or that he is so dull and stupid, that he can't see the Blessing proffer'd him, and therefore altogether unworthy her least Regard, or future Notice.

I have two lovers; the first is very entertaining, but somewhat positive; the latter very dull, but prodigiously complaisant. Now the case is, sir, which had I best to take? I love wit mightily, but then I hate to be contradicted; I love complaisance, but then I hate dullness. I know not how to determine; therefore as two heads are better than one, Dear Sir, a line from you would settle the anxiety of

Estelle Weathercock.

Madam, if after marriage you would willingly condescend to be govern'd take the wit; if you chuse rather to govern, take the fool.

Nestor Druid.

THE CENTINEL, JULY 23RD, 1757

Mr. Centinel, Though your superior good sense may set you above the influence of those tender follies which so frequently bring misfortunes on my sex, yet I will suppose you have a heart full of commiseration for woes you are incapable of feeling, and in that confidence will presume to intreat your advice in an accident which has involved in the greatest perplexities a young person, who otherwise might have been happy to the fullest extent of all her wishes.

I am, sir, the sole daughter and heiress of a gentleman of eight hundred pounds per annum. I lost my mother in my very early years; but the extreme tenderness of my father towards me left me no sense of that misfortune. About ten months ago I happened into the acquaintance of a young gentleman, who, according to my opinion, has every requisite not only to please, but to command the respect of all who know him. He made his addresses to me; but very privately, as his estate is somewhat inferior to that I was born to enjoy. My father, however, was so much taken with his person, character and behaviour, that it was at last agreed between us he should venture to declare his passion, and implore his sanction to our loves: but, alas! just at the time this was resolved upon, that dear parent was seized with a violent fever, of which he died in a few days, and left me under the guardianship of his brother.

Here, sir, began my calamities; the funeral obsequies were no sooner over than my uncle proposed a marriage between me and the son of his wife by a former husband; a gentleman in whom, if I was not prepossessed in favour of another, I could find nothing to approve. I will not trouble you with the shock this discourse gave me; but resolving to put an end, if possible, to all farther sollicitations on this score, I freely confessed to him that my heart and vows were already engaged to another; on which he flew into a great rage, told me, it did not become a maid of my age to chuse for herself; that he thought his son-in-law was every way worthy of me; and in fine, that he was determined I should either marry him or nobody.

The distraction I was in, and which still hangs upon me, is not to be expressed: sensible of the power the late cruel law has given him over me, I have tried every means to soften his obdurate heart, have had recourse to tears and complaints, have remonstrated to him how unhappy even the person, whose interest he espoused, must be in marrying a woman who never could be brought to love, or even like him; and how inhuman it would be to separate two hearts linked together by the strictest ties of mutual love. But all this has not the least effect, my uncle is wholly governed by his wife, and I am every day compelled to endure the double persecution of their importunities, and the nauseous addresses of the man I hate.

My lover, who is all despair, talks of nothing but obliging his rival to resign either his pretensions or his life; my tears, persuasions and commands have alone hitherto prevented the rash attempt; how long they will have any force I know not, and I am every hour trembling for the consequence.

I am now but two months turned of eighteen, and sure it is utterly impossible for me to support, for near three whole years, this load of anguish, which, instead of diminishing, gains every moment some addition to its weight. My lover would fain prevail on me to suffer him to have recourse to some needy clergyman, for a sum of money, to privately join our hands; but though I as earnestly desire this union as himself can do, yet I confess I have not courage to enter into it this way.

Pity, sir, I beseech you, the agonies I suffer for the mischief which has already happened to me, and the dreadful apprehensions of the yet worse that may befall me; and if it be in the power of wit or reason to extricate me from the miseries I am at present plunged in, exert those charming qualities for the relief of one who will always retain a due sense of the obligation. In the mean time, be assured I am, with the great respect,

> *Sir, your most humble and*
> *most obedient servant,*
> *AMELIA.*

I am extremely affected with poor AMELIA'S case; but dare say there are at this instant ten thousand of his majesty's subjects who labour under the same unhappy situation. This, however, is no consolation to a person of a generous way of thinking, and it is only from her own fortitude, patience and resolution, she can hope relief.

Severe as the late marriage-act has been accounted, it binds not for ever; the shackles it hangs upon the heart will of themselves fall off in time; dear one and twenty will at last arrive, and young ladies will then be at liberty to pursue their wishes.

Nothing can be truly called a calamity to which we can see an end; I hope therefore the good sense Amelia is mistress of, will enable her to consider that this decree of the legislature only delays, not frustrates the consummation of her happiness, and assured that an hour will come in which she will have it in her own power to triumph over the obduracy of her uncle, bear rather with indifference and contempt than grief, the little teasings she may 'till then sustain from his importunities.

Besides, though she knows and beholds with horror the length of the chain by which she is bound, yet she knows not what events fortune may have in store to shorten it; her uncle may die; the young spark grow weary of prosecuting an unsuccessful suit, and drop it of himself; a thousand accidents may happen to ease her of this part of her vexation.

The greatest difficulty which, according to my opinion, this lady has to combat with, is to restrain the impatience of her lover from breaking into actions which, in all probability would more effectually than the late act has power to do, put a total period to all their hopes.

I am very sensible that the fire of youth, especially in our sex, when agitated by any violent passion, is wild, ungovernable, deaf to all remonstrance, sets everything at defiance, and a lover debarred, like this gentleman, the enjoyment of his wishes, is ready, when any advice is offered him, to cry out with the poet,

No law is made for love;
Law is to things which to free choice relate:
Love is not in our choice, but in our fate.
Laws are but positive; love's power, we see,
In nature's sanction, and her first decree.

But if the gentleman in question can have so much command over himself, as to forbear seeking that satisfaction which he may imagine both his love and honour demand for this intrusion on his rights; yet may these rivals, who doubtless are equally incensed against each other, by some accident meet together, words may arise between them, the swords may come for second course, and there is no event more dreadful than what may justly be apprehended from such rencounter.

I cannot therefore help thinking, but that it would be a very prudent expedient for this favourite lover to pass the time of his deprivation either in the country or some foreign part: such proper methods might be taken as to prevent any interception of the letters between them; they might lay open their whole souls to each other every post, and enjoy a more undisturbed felicity than any they can expect to find amidst the snares, plots and artifices that may be put in practise by those whose interest it is to divide their loves. But above all, I would fain corroborate the resolution Amelia seems to have taken, never to sacrifice her honour and the interest of her future family to a too hasty gratification of her passion; as there was some short time since a clergyman of the church of England under sentence of transportation for an offence of this nature, I should be sorry to see another of that sacred robe dragged like a common felon to the bar of a court of judicature.

THE MATRON

... *The indelicate freedom some women allow themselves in conversation, to the evident distress of the more reserved, I think justly merits reprehension. Does any age or state authorize a woman to lay aside every delicate female grace, and allow her to hazard expressions that wound the ear of modesty? Surely none. ... I was lately in company with several ladies and gentlemen, when the former, by their indelicacy, were the means of rendering the conversation so insupportable that – though a married woman – I was under the necessity of retiring, overwhelmed with confusion; and unless your salutary advice, madam, is attended with success, shall be obliged to drop further intercourse with several families, among whom are some worthy characters.*

– Maria Townsend.

The Matron cannot but approve the sentiments contained in the above epistle. . . . A licentious, bold female, indecent in her expressions, loose and forward in her manners, is entitled to no respect either from man or woman. . . . Often I am surprised, in spite of repeated observation, to see the forward, audacious airs which many women assume, women in the highest ranks of life. . . . 'Want of decency,' says an ingenious writer, 'is want of sense'; and surely his observation is not confined to his own sex. . . .

D.W.B.E.—C

A few years ago, I married a very pretty girl, from pure affection alone, as she had nothing to bring me but her pleasing person and good disposition. . . . During the last two years we frequented the camps . . . and during that time it became the fashion among the ladies of the officers to appear in riding habits. This mode of dress was, probably, quite convenient for them, and not totally out of character; but surely there was no reason for this mode's extending to all classes of females because it suited one of them? But so it has been . . . my wife . . . whips on her habit as soon as she gets out of bed, sets down to breakfast in her beaver, and goes to market in her boots. She appears, indeed, in no other dress till towards evening, then all close covering is thrown off, and she sallies forth in a large bell-hoop, low stays, and so transparent a piece of drapery is thrown over her bosom that it discovers what it attempts, apparently, to conceal. She is so enclosed from head to foot all day when she is with me, that I cannot see a single charm lower than her chin. At seven or eight in the evening she is quite undressed for company and every man who falls in her way has an opportunity to gaze on those beauties which are exhibited for the observation of all men. . . . My dear madam, say something very strong against these glaring absurdities and you will exceedingly oblige,

Your humble servant, W.G.

The Matron . . . subscribes to his sentiments, yet not being willing to seem particularly severe upon any mode of dress which so many ladies have adopted, she thinks that single ladies, if they find the riding habit more compact and convenient, may wear it uncensured and unmolested. When they become wives they will, if they are truly wise, wear only those dresses which are most becoming in the eyes of their husbands. . . .

... *My father, dear, good man, has, for some time, wanted to have me married; and merely, as far as I can find, for the charming satisfaction of having grandchildren. Several matches have been proposed, but the men, that is to say, their estates, did not answer expectations. At length, however, an old friend's nephew was brought forward, my father thinking that the numbers of his acres was sufficient. . . . Such a popinjay, such a puppy, was introduced, that I felt myself absolutely disgusted at the sight. My lover (that is, my nominal lover, for he seemed to have too much of the Narcissus about him, to love me or any woman under the sun) was dressed in maroon coloured tabinet coat, and breeches trimed with silver lace and spangles; his waistcoat was white satin, embroidered with foils, etc. His hair was dressed to the extremity of the fashion, and so loaded with Marechal that I was almost ready to faint, to sink under the powerful smell. He had also a large bourquet of jonquils, orange flowers, etc. His hands were as white as curds, and loaded with rings of an enormous size; his two watches hung with chains and trinkets without number, so that he could not move without making them rattle in the most disagreeable manner. His buckles totally covered his shoes, and almost blinded me with their brilliancy. Such was the figure whom I am to love, honour, and obey. . . .*

Harriet Hedges

P.S. I cannot help informing you that I received the pretty creature in my riding-habit; the contrast, therefore, was curious and complete.

... When a man marries, he has much more important business to attend to than the care of his dress; his wife, his children, the improvement and proper management of his fortune. . . . When a woman has the misfortune to be united to coxcomb, to whom can she look up for support? To whom can she communicate all her sorrows and all her joys? From a man wholly under the influence of a raging passion for outward appearance, she can expect no feelings on her account. . . . Mrs. Grey, therefore, hopes that Mr. Hedges will consent to his daughter's refusing the present offer. She advices the amiable Harriet, at the same time, to lay aside her riding-habit, when she is not actually going to mount her horse, as her next admirer may, perhaps, feel as strong an aversion to a masculine lady, as she herself feels to an effeminate gentleman.

. . . Do, Spec., recommend me to the ladies! For I don't know how it is, I have not the audacity enough to introduce myself. This diffidence may proceed from not knowing the world; however, I do not much regret it, as I am in possession of that which is always pleasing to the ladies, sentiment. . . . Acquaint me of the most certain method to secure the propitious smiles of the fair ladies. . . .

'Graces! graces!' *They* form the ladies' talisman. And as for sentimental hypocrisy, a sensible woman will always treat it with contempt.

THE NEW SPECTATOR, APRIL 20TH, 1784

My wife is gone mad! — and, what is worse, politically mad! Ever since the commencement of the Westminster election, my wife has been intoxicated with politics, my servants with strong beer, myself with vexation, and my house has resounded with nothing but 'Fox for ever!' It would have been some consolation had she confined her folly to her own house, but alas! she has been making a fool of herself all over the town! She has been canvassing with a vengeance! And what with palming one fellow, kissing another and coaxing with thousands has driven me almost horn-mad! . . . Her reputation is indeed unimpeached, and I believe her present conduct arises solely from the singularity she always assumes and which is her chief, if not her only fault. But she should remember that female reputation is of slender contexture; and that

'*To her belongs
The care to shun the blast of sland'rous tongues.*'

This, however, is impossible so long as she interferes in matters which by no means concern her or her sex. . . .

The gentleman very justly calls himself a *fond* husband: he is indeed too fond and too indulgent in permitting his wife to disgrace herself by a conduct so reprehensible. . . . If reasoning fails, he should then recourse to remonstrance; and should that also fail, he should hurry her into the country and by taking her from the scene of action, endeavour to reclaim her. It has, of late years, been too much the vogue amongst the fashionable fair to imitate in everything the other sex, particularly in modes of dress and matters of amusement. . . .

LADY'S MAGAZINE, 1786

. . . I have been talked to, admired and complimented for my beauty these five years but though I am just arrived to the age of nineteen see not the smallest prospect of being suited. . . . To make the matter a thousand times worse, I have had the galling mortification to see above half a dozen of my most intimate friends, the ugliest girls you can conceive, settled perfectly to their satisfaction. What a deal of pains have I taken to improve my face and my shape! But if you cannot put me in a way to make something of myself after all, I will actually unfrizzle my hair, throw my rouge into the fire; stuff a cushion with my bustle, press down my handkerchief to my bosom, and, in short, appear exactly as nature has made me. . . .

Harriet Hasty.

. . . A modest compliance with the fashion in some degree will be very proper and we imagine that most men like to see their wives make a genteel appearance, which may certainly be done with no great expense. . . . As to rouge, no woman in the world should have anything to do with it. Nature requires no such daubing to render her amiable. If Miss Hasty therefore will trust to Nature alone, she will not be at much expense or trouble; consequently, she will stand a better chance of being settled, as men in general are not pleased with any incumbrance and often inclined to think that the woman would be a sufficient one without her wardrobe. . . .

I am one of those unfortunate beings who have resigned the stall out of their own hands and are therefore in danger of falling to the ground; or in other words I have given my children an education so much above myself that they despise my opinion and ridicule my appearance. . . . For my own part, though I am no scholar, yet I can read, cast accounts and write very well; and when I was only nine years old the curate of our parish gave me half-a-crown for reading the tenth chapter of Nehemiah without even spelling a single word. But as to reading the bible now-a-days, Mrs Mentor, that, my children tell me, is quite out of fashion. *. . . My daughters, to be sure, are very fond of reading; but then it is not only novels, or books that teach them to be indolent and undutiful. And it was but yesterday that Selina told me a good head was better than a good heart; and that though I had been the means of bringing her into the world yet she had not required it of me, and therefore did not consider it as an obligation. . . . If you will but give those still dear, but misguided girls a hint in your next number of the misery they occasion their affectionate parents we shall be ever bound.*

Sarah Congor.

To the young ladies I must enquire by what strange and sophisticated mode of reasoning they have discovered that parents have no right to expect either duty, gratitude, respect or love from beings whose very lives would have terminated at their birth but for that fostering tenderness with which they watched the helpless state of infancy. . . . Can they suppose that an enlightened mind will try to break every human tie and bid defiance to the laws of Heaven? . . . Alas! they know not that the curse of Heaven descends on those who wound a parent's heart!

CAROLINE DEL.   K.S.BRANSTON SC.

1815–1868

AS REVOLUTIONARY ardour died in Europe, so did the independent, immoral ardour among English woman. In a sickening about-turn they not only returned to base but added an almost impregnable barrier between themselves and the opposite sex. This barrier, dented but still standing for nearly a hundred years, is scrupulously supported by the growing number of magazine Aunt Aggies, who are kept busy proscribing the limited approach allowed through it.

And in her little enclave, the middle-class woman was left with one aim, to become the kind of perfect lady extolled in a magazine: 'She is a being of delicate perceptions, tremblingly alive to the least infringement of decorum; ever studying to please by unostentatious candour and heartfelt benevolence, anxious to make all around her easy and happy, polite without ceremony, modest without bashfulness, commanding all sorts of attention by her retiring and unasking lowliness, and with a humble, heartfelt piety.'

TO THE MATRON

I am nineteen, have had a boarding school education, speak French tolerably well; play the piano in some style; dance, draw, and do ornamental needlework. My papa is a haberdasher and he wants me to stand in his shop; and I wish to ask you whether I ought? And what is the use of an education like mine, if, instead of making an advantage of it, I am to forget it all, by mixing with shop men-and-women, and measuring tape like a dowdy? My mama says it is wrong, and as my papa can give me very little fortune, he ought to exhibit me as much as possible with all my accomplishments; the only chance I have of moving in my proper sphere, by getting a rich husband.

If your education has been sound, you will not lose it by mixing with the shop-women, and measuring tape; and you will not appear like a *dowdy*, when, by assisting your father, you are endeavouring to make some return for his indulgence. I have omitted shop*men*, because I think a young lady of such a mind as yours appears to be might be in some danger among them. . . . I appear severe, I dare say; but, my dear simple girl, listen to me – your education, if it consists of no more than you have related, has been merely ornamental, and that, without the useful, is detrimental instead of serviceable; and will never procure you a husband to make you happy, without you endeavour to connect with it the more estimable qualities of the mind. . . .

As you profess to be the director, I hope you will also prove to be the defender, of your sex and advocate the cause of a numerous body of us . . . I mean that generally and illiberally stigmatized class called Old Maids.

Many of us . . . become so not from any fault of our own, but from many of those causes which militate against female action and female advancement. I will instance myself. I am of respectable, though not rich, parents; my face and form were thought more than passable; and my understanding . . . equalled that of many young ladies who have gained husbands. . . . But I had no fortune, and as gentlemen now look for wives who may be the means of best assisting them in supporting a style, *rather than in regulating a family, I lost many offers I might have had. . . . No, my dear Matron, do hold up the rod of our tormentors. . . . We Old Maids are certainly entitled to consideration from our usefulness in society; we serve to fill up corners in company . . . we assist conversation when a pause will permit us to presume with a remark . . . an Old Maid makes one at a dance when an odd one is wanted to complete the set. . . . To such and many more mortifications we submit for a quiet life . . . the stronger sex should certainly have the generosity to allow for the failings of the weaker, and defend them from insult, not treat them with neglect. . . .*

SARAH SPINSTER.

The Matron sincerely sympathizes with all who are in the same predicament with Miss Spinster; however, she thinks Miss S's remarks carried a *little too far,* though in many respects very true. . . . Perhaps, if properly analyzed, there is not a more admirable character in society than an Old Maid – become so through dignified prudence, innate modesty, and self command; who has subdued passion by reason, and inclination by duty; suppressed affection when propriety forbade its encouragement; borne deprivation with fortitude, and mortification with cheerfulness. To effect this demands more powers than to make conquests, as it requires less to glare than to illumine.

Popping the question. W.Y. There are many ways of accomplishing this delicate matter. No specific rules can be laid down. The method must be modified by the circumstances of each case. Do you wed for love, or money? or are you slightly quickened by the former, yet eager for the latter? Have you a fortune to bestow on your bride? Or do you want a good homely dame, to make your toast and mend your stockings? Are you a youth, urged on by the irrepressible promptings of first love, or a widower with three small children? The circumstances suggested necessarily influence your mode of asking. . . . If, however, you wish to make the matter a commercial transaction, the honest way will be to give it that appearance at once – strike your balance-sheet, and, laying it before her, ask hers in return. Having thus taken stock, you may propose a partnership. . . .

FAMILY FRIEND, 1850

Can there be a case in which a lady may, without overstepping the limits of modesty, allow a gentleman to know that she has a preference for him – in short, can you tell me a method in which a lady might propose *to a gentleman of whose admiration and esteem she is sure, but who does not entertain feelings of a warmer sort, or from his position does not presume to show them? I am about 21 and have always been considered diffident and timid. What can I do? You, as a gentleman, can tell what a gentleman would think.*   *A.B.*

We know of no 'method' by which a lady may 'propose' to a gentleman without overstepping the limits of propriety. Such proposals, even if successful, are ever dangerous to love. They beget an independence in the man which soon wanes into indifference and becomes the bane of married life. If however a lady's attentions are strongly fixed, there are many gentle and becoming ways of attracting love – not of declaring it. But the utmost caution must be observed. . . .

FAMILY FRIEND, 1850

Flirting. F.C. Conduct unbecoming the true modesty of woman, and particularly a flirtatious and coquettish demeanour towards the male sex, comes under this denomination. It is an error in conduct against which ladies should rigidly guard. Few things will more easily and rapidly lower the lady who practises it in the estimation of all who surround her.

Will you have the kindness to inform me, whether it is considered a correct thing for a young lady to bring down her nightcaps to work in the drawing room, in the presence of a young gentleman who is staying in the house. M.B.P.

Perhaps there is no great impropriety in the young lady's doing so; but it is not an evidence of good taste, and had better be avoided.

FAMILY FRIEND, 1852

J.D. We agree with you that the domestic manners and vulgarities of some of the male portion of our youth are frequently very far from claiming our admiration. . . . The expression 'like a brick' is an absurdity, although it has a meaning when taken in conjunction with the appearance and expression of the utterer, who is usually a sort of made-up gentleman that walks in a sphere between the vulgar and the genteel. . . . Such metaphors as these take their rise, generally, by accident, and become part of the 'unwashed' vernacular, which we hope is never heard amongst the readers of the *Family Friend*.

LADIES TREASURY, 1858

Pamela says she is a young governess in a noble family and that one of the younger sons, an 'Honourable' (as the poor simple girl proudly says), is in love with her. He has owned to her that were he to marry her, he would be turned out into the world a beggar, but yet he threatens suicide if she refuses to allow him to address her clandestinely as a lover! 'Pamela' must run the risk (no very great one) of her lover's destroying himself, else he will destroy her. She must leave her situation at once. Her situation is one of great and immediate danger. If this clandestine attachment is discovered she will lose, not only her situation, but her character.

Elvira thinks she had reason to be 'dreadfully shocked' because the servant 'let in upon her' one of her fashionable female friends while she was mending stockings. We disagree with Elvira and assure her that there is nothing more paltry in ladies than the fear of having it known that they employ themselves in household affairs.

LADIES TREASURY, 1858

A Spinster has heard a most eloquent and inspiring sermon on the subject of woman's influence. She asks us whether it would be too forward in her to write to the clergyman for further advice and direction. There is no indiscretion in 'A Spinster's' writing to the preacher, if she is clear in her own mind that it is the wish for improvement, and not a personal interest in the speaker, that urges her to attempt opening a correspondence.

HOME MAGAZINE, AUGUST 28TH, 1858

Afflicted Father. Your case is truly a terrible one, as unregenerate human nature goes; but a man who is willing to do by his own erring and ruined daughter as he would have his Heavenly Father do by him, would not have much difficulty in deciding upon his course, under such circumstances as you are placed in. Think of your daughter's former goodness and innocence – of the great love you bore her, and which she so ardently returned – of her youth, her ignorance of the wiles of the world, her loving and trusting heart, and above all, of the downward course and awful doom which inevitably await her unless she is shielded from such a fate under some protecting roof, and in some pure family circle. You should yield to your wife's entreaties, and receive the erring one back into the asylum of home. A mother's affections and instincts are as near divine as anything human can be, and should be allowed to govern in such cases.

W.C. If the girl loves you, and you love her, we see no reason why the fact of her having corresponded with another young man should prevent your marrying her.

LADIES TREASURY, 1859

Lucy says she is 19 and is reckoned very pretty . . . yet she only has two admirers. One is 22, an author, with a debt of £18 for the printing of his book. The other a stockbroker of 62 who would keep Lucy a carriage and pair. We advise Lucy to marry the stockbroker; it is better to be an old man's darling than a young man's slave. . . .

HOME MAGAZINE, JANUARY 26TH, 1859

L.N. Any man who will ask a girl to do what he knows her mother would disapprove of, is an unsafe companion for her, and should be avoided. No gentleman or man of any principle and honour would do such a thing. As to the matter you have mentioned, our advice is that you at once tell the whole case to your mother, and then strictly follow her advice.

HOME MAGAZINE, NOVEMBER 11TH, 1859

Charlotte. The conduct of your lover is very equivocal. He professes the warmest attachment, and seeks for a suitable return from you, but refuses to solicit the approbation of your parents. This is extremely suspicious, and coupled with his conduct in the drawing room, warrants us in concluding that his motives are not at all honourable.

I am acquainted with a young lady who seems to take pleasure in my society, and yet never invites me into the house when I accompany her home from church. I have waited upon other ladies, but that has no effect. What shall I do?

In the first place you should learn that young ladies, who set a proper estimate upon themselves, are not in the habit of inviting gentlemen into their abodes unless they are very intimate family friends.

LADIES TREASURY, 1860

A lady of thirty-five, well-born, well-bred, and once very well off, but now without a home, may well be doubtful respecting the propriety of her accepting the offer of a wealthy old widower of 68, to live with him as a daughter. . . . She says she lives at present at a boarding-school, where she has sole charge of the wardrobe of thirty young ladies; has all the mending to do, and the junior pupils to wash, dress and teach. Her life, she says, is one of isolation, unprogressive labour, and great responsibility. She has to rise at five in summer, and six in winter; and though always at her post, is only paid £15 per annum, and never cherished by one kind word or little attention. . . . But once openly living in a questionable position, once the mark of public censure and slander, she is in quarantine for life. Society never forgives any woman for defying its opinions and disobeying its laws. . . .

THE HOME MAGAZINE, AUGUST 15TH, 1860

Estelle. This young lady says she is blessed with wise and excellent parents, but she thinks they are a little too strict in obliging her lover to take his leave of her every evening at ten precisely. We do not agree with Estelle. Ten o'clock is quite late enough. The common practice of leaving young girls to sit up with their lovers alone, is one which we utterly detest, and believe to be immoral and injurious.

'The wood violet' would like to know the amount of encouragement she may, with propriety, give to a gentleman who pays her
great attention. . . . We will tell her what delicate and indirect
encouragement we think a modest maiden can give to an un-
declared suitor without in the least degree derogating from that
dignity and feminine reserve which we delight to uphold. She
may always welcome him with smiles, and a cordial shake of the
hand. She may ask his opinion as to the books she should read,
and the songs she should sing. She might ascertain what style of
hair dressing, what colours, patterns, and mode of dress he
prefers, and adopt them.

LADIES TREASURY, JULY, 1860

Snowdrop. Marrying for love is no indication of madness; but
if the man you love is unworthy of that sentiment, then you are
not likely to promote your happiness by marrying him. It is on
character, sympathy, and a variety of causes, that wedded happiness depends. Sometimes very happy matches are made late
in life, sometimes by those in the morning of existence; but as
you question us on the subject, we give it as our opinion, that 20
for a young lady, and 25 for a gentleman, are about the best ages
for entering upon matrimony, and we think the gentleman should
generally be a few years older than the lady. We do not approve
of marrying merely for 'talent, money or beauty'. People should
marry with a view of promoting their mutual happiness, and of
making themselves more useful members of society, and of rendering themselves more capable of performing their duty to their
Maker and to their fellow-creatures.

EVERY WEEK, NOVEMBER 8TH, 1862

Clarrisa asks: 'What harm is there in an innocent flirtation?'
First, may we ask what 'innocent flirtation' is? A flirtation can
never be innocent unless a wanton and deliberate trifling with the
holiest feelings of the human heart be so. Of all games, it is the
most dangerous, not so much because it may break hearts as that
it may ruin the honour and happiness of those concerned.
Coquetry in a woman is equivalent to libertinism in a man.

EVERY WEEK, NOVEMBER IST, 1862

A.A.A. (Truro). Embroidered shirt-fronts are an affectation. It has been well described as a sign of degenerate taste when a man puts on a breast-plate of fine muslin embroidery or lace insertion. The finest, the whitest, the most costly of linen, the neatest, the most faultlessly regular, the tiniest of all little tucks, if you like; all this is very right and proper; but the lace insertion and muslin embroidery is a hideous mistake.

LADIES TREASURY, 1863

A Fiancée. Abstain from exaggerated expressions of affection in your letters. Let your lover have always something to hope for, let him not discover all your love. With men it is the pursuit of an object which makes their happiness. . . .

HOME MAGAZINE, NOVEMBER 28TH, 1863

Mary would like to know if it is proper for a strange gentleman to commence a conversation with a lady he doesn't know, in an omnibus. No gentleman would take such a liberty with a lady whose conduct showed that she respected herself. Contemptuous silence is the best reproof for such impertinence.

LADIES TREASURY, 1863

Emma. If you had daily employment of thinking and working you would not be so unhappy. Thought without work is idleness; work without thought is weary labour. The two united produce the gem of contentment.

D.W.B.I.—D

Elouise. You tell us that you are in love with a very bashful young gentleman. You inquire whether you had better try to cure him of his timidity and bring him to a declaration. We think you have no right to monopolize such a natural curiosity in this age as 'a bashful young man'. Put him in a glass case and show him round the country as a specimen of an extinct race. It would pay well.

FAMILY FRIEND, MARCH, 1864

Hysterics. Dr. March says the best cure for hysterics is to discharge the servant-girl. In his opinion, there is nothing like brisk exercise and useful occupation to keep the nervous system from becoming unstrung. Some women think they want a physician, he says, when they only need a scrubbing brush.

ENGLISHWOMAN'S DOMESTIC MAGAZINE, 1865

As to proposing, *Amelia,* well you cannot make a man propose if he wont and tantalising it is and aggravating, very. You talk with him, walk with him, dance with him, flirt with him, dress for him, sing to him, agree with him, worry, and still he holds out, Giant Obdurate. You are very much in love with him indeed. That is a pity. Otherwise our advice would be, cast him off for ever. As it is, we think you would be quite warranted in getting papa to speak to him, but you know, there is a risk. 'Excuse me, Mr. Obdurate,' says papa in his blandest manner, but with a great deal of determination, too – 'excuse me, but I have observed of late etc. etc. etc., – daughter's feelings, etc. etc. etc. May I ask your intentions?' 'Bless your heart!' says Obdurate. 'I have no intentions whatever – never dreamed of such a thing!' Awkward this – very.

Annie. Decidedly not; do not for a moment suppose that because a young gentleman asks you for your photograph that he intends making you his wife. But above all things, never give the photograph; you do not know what use may be made of it.

LADIES TREASURY, 1865

Alice F. You should never have been permitted to form acquaintance with any one so much beneath your own position. Your friends will cast you off, and your husband perhaps despise you.

THE HOME MAGAZINE, FEBRUARY 21ST, 1866

Lydia. Of course a lady should thank a gentleman for picking up her handkerchief, or book, or handing her a glass of water, or for performing any act of kindness or politeness. She need not *speak* her thanks, but may smile or bow them. A *look* of appreciation may be far more satisfactory than formal words of thanks.

LADIES TREASURY, APRIL 1ST, 1866

Prudence. The custom of kissing or being kissed in a game of forfeits, is rather to be reprehended than encouraged in a mixed assemblage. When the visitors only consist of relatives, it is another matter, perhaps, nothing is thought of it; but it must be pleasanter for any pure minded girl to feel that her lips have been kept intact from rude embraces. . . .

THE HOME MAGAZINE, JULY 25TH, 1866

Tom Lee. A young lady who declines your company should not receive presents from you. Young women who accept presents from young men promiscuously are hardly expected to make the best of wives.

G.J.B. should not be too ready to suppose that a young lady's manifesting gay and lively manners is an indication, as he says, that 'she wants to get herself into his favour'. Unless a young lady is very foolish, forward or ridiculous, she is not likely to make a very alarming assault on a young man. For she must (or ought to) know that obtrusive manners and levity disgust rather than win a sensible man. To be sure, there is a plentiful crop of noodles in the world; and if it be true that every Jack has his Jill, some ridiculous love-making on both sides must occur. We hope these remarks apply neither to our correspondent nor the merry young lady.

H.F. Do not think of advertising for a wife. No girl worth having would respond to such an invitation. You seem as yet not to have met with the right young lady. Wait a little longer; she will most likely come in time. Girls do not wear their hearts upon their sleeves, but wait with graceful diffidence for the wooer to come to them. It is probably your own fault that you have not made yourself sufficiently agreeable to draw forth an exhibition of those qualities which are best adapted to kindle the flame of love.

Into 1900

NO ONE can remain in a state of siege without the strain beginning to tell, and the Victorian woman was no exception. To compensate for submerged sexual and intellectual desires she had tried religion; she now turned to exercise and drink as well. The magazines always approved the first palliative wholeheartedly, the second after some reservations, and of course came down like thunder on the third. Modern psychiatrists see another indication of sexual frustration in the mothers' strict physical punishment of their children.

Blinkered as they were, the magazines fought tenaciously against any other widening of a woman's sphere. 'Young ladies should not be on the look-out for profitable employment but should leave that for their humbler sisters; we have a horror of strong-minded women. Surely there are enough of domestic duties to give women all the scope needed for their abilities.'

But towards the end of the century a phenomenon called The Modern Girl made her appearance. 'The Modern Girl is dutiful though she is apt to give her parents counsel and reproof; sometimes she has views on politics. . . . She knows quite well what she is about and is absolutely sincere in her likes and dislikes which she is apt to express with considerable candour.'

Women had gradually eased their way into the professions and higher education; they had talked and fought endlessly for political rights. Although not directly involved, the stolid, puritan middle-class could not help but be influenced by the air of feminine advancement. The Aunt Aggies are not asked to cope with outright rebellion, but there is a hint of protest from some readers.

43

AN ENGLISH MAMA

Many naughty children are only to be startled into better conduct by sudden corporal punishment. In your case we advise you at the first act of disobedience to adminster a sharp box on the ear or *hard* slap; if this fails, have recourse to the remedy you propose, but be sure it is severe, and in the old-fashioned style; a good birch of twigs hurts more and injures less than the hand or rod. If a 'good sound whipping' fails you are in a worse plight than before, and school is the only chance of breaking in a troublesome girl. Absence from home and school trials and hardship have wrought wonders.

OCTOBER, 1868

I . . . followed your advice implicitly; that very morning, when my daughter was disobedient, I gave her a box on the ear. This seemed to have little or no effect. In the evening she was just as obstinate as ever, so I took her into my room and just raised her dress, and gave her three or four smart slaps, which, through her underclothing, she could hardly feel, but having the semblance of a 'good sound whipping' I thought it might frighten her into obedience, and so it did for a day or two, but after that she became just as bad as ever. I then obtained a 'good birch of twigs' and showed it to her and told her that she would be soundly whipped with it if she continued her disobedience. The next day, forgetful of the warning, she was as bad as ever. I told her to go to my room and wait till I came. I waited for about half an hour, as I had no wish to punish her in anger, but wished to think over the matter coolly. I made her take off her trousers in order that she might feel the chastisement sharply. I then put her across my knee in 'the old-fashioned style' and gave her about twenty sharp strokes of the birch, then told her to dress herself, stating the punishment was at an end, and there would be no further disgrace. But I also told her that whenever she disobeyed again whipping would be according to the fault, more or less severely. The effect, I must tell you, was magical; for three days afterwards I could not have had a better child. . . . Since September I have had to use it a great many times, but as time has gone on I found a longer lapse has occurred between each punishment, so that in the course of time I hope to do without it altogether. . . .

44

On the subject of discipline for girls allow me to state that we had a niece of fifteen to educate who was of a very disobedient and determined temperament and who is now being brought to a sense of duty and obedience through occasionally smart whippings with the birch-rod administered by her governess at a strict boarding school. This lady has a large school of fifty pupils; she is firm in her discipline when once she makes up her mind to punish, and maintains that the rod is the only proper and most effective remedy for girls of any age when naughty. I am quite opposed to long impositions, confinements, etc., as practised in some schools of the present day, and quite think that where the stubborn will of the girl requires to be brought into subjection, no means are so efficacious as the judicious use of the birch. . . .

FEBRUARY, 1869

GENTLENESS . . . was surprised to read of the gentle treatment used by the so-called English Mamma. She should think those mammas must have the nigger blood in them, and they are practising slaves' treatment on their children to their own delight and love of beating. How can the cowardly tyrants who use the whipping on their children bear to call themselves English? All her friends who are mothers unite in saying that such a course of treatment brings the children to being deceitful, ungrateful, and hypocritical.

THE HOME MAGAZINE, MAY 2ND, 1866

Repentant. 'Youthful indiscretions', as they are ludicrously termed, seldom go unpunished; but, as we presume, from the tenor of your letter, that the love you bore the cook was only too warm, we don't see why you should go forth into the world characterless. There surely were some extenuating circumstances, and our advice to you is, remain at home, for if you went to sea at your age you would only be rated as a 'lubber', and, to use a vulgar adage, 'receive more kicks than pence'.

Ellen complains sadly that she is not permitted to do as she likes. Perhaps it would be better for most of us if we could not. Papa insists upon the family *all* appearing at the breakfast table at eight o'clock in the morning. Nothing but illness will be accepted as an excuse, and, as Ellen ingenuously remarks, one cannot be always playing the invalid soldier. Mamma submits to papa entirely – that is to say, acting as she pleases, so far as she herself is concerned. She does not 'stand up' for her daughters, and papa's 'homilies' on idleness are 'a dreadful bore'! We counsel Ellen to listen patiently and to follow papa's wishes. Getting up early in the morning can do her no harm. She knows the old rhyme, of course, with regard to the amount of hours' sleep needed:

> Nature requires five,
> Custom takes seven,
> Laziness takes nine,
> And wickedness eleven!

Going to bed, as a rule, at half-past ten, and being too tired to rise to an eight o'clock breakfast, is preposterous.

SOURCE UNKNOWN, 1871

I have borne for twenty-two years with all humility and gentleness of spirit all the insults of a coarse nature. I have been a devoted slave to the man I swore to love and obey. I have borne insults and hard work and words without a murmur, but my blood boils when I see my gentle innocent girls tremble at the sound of their father's voice. . . .

As he is the breadwinner you must bear it with a meek and quiet spirit. . . .

If the Editor will excuse her, Kate would like to inform Theodosia that very few people would think she had been guilty of an impropriety in giving a pair of slippers to a young man to whom she was not engaged.

A sister writes. The opinion advanced by Kate on the subject of gifts to young men is so subversive of maidenly modesty, that really it ought not to pass unchallenged. I can assure Kate that she is very much mistaken in supposing that *most* well educated young ladies, or that *any* good mother of a family of girls would agree with her. It would be a sore pity if society has come to such a pass that the Editor should stand unsupported in the 'Drawing Room' of the 'Young Englishwoman' in protecting against one of the 'fastest' innovations of this 'fast' age. All the rules of etiquette and propriety must be set at defiance before a young lady is free to *offer* gifts and attentions to a young gentleman, instead of *receiving* them from him according to the established rules of courtship.

THE YOUNG ENGLISHWOMAN, JANUARY, 1875

Bessie Lawer inquires, if a gentleman were playing the accompaniment of a lady's song, would it be proper for the lady to turn over the music. (The gentleman should, if possible, turn over the music.)

THE YOUNG ENGLISHWOMAN, MAY, 1875

Mary asks if a young gentleman desired a kiss from a young lady, should she comply with his wishes at once, or not? (I should say not, unless the young lady and young gentleman were engaged to be married to each other.) *What excuse could she make if in want of one?* (No excuse would be necessary, since it is not usual for young ladies to kiss young gentlemen whenever they ask. If it were, they would always be asking.) *And if she gave the kiss would she be thought fast?* (Her lady friends would think so, and say so. Her gentlemen friends would think so, but perhaps would not say so.) *And if she refused, would she be thought rude?* (No, for it is the gentleman who is rude to ask it.)

THE YOUNG ENGLISHWOMAN, 1872

Ladies usually give a distant bow on meeting any gentleman once introduced to them; it will not be difficult to show by your manner that it is a bow of *recognition*, not acquaintance. . . .

THE YOUNG ENGLISHWOMAN, JANUARY, 1875

Alma would be much obliged if the Editor of the Young Englishwoman would answer the following questions through the medium of that valuable journal: When Alma is walking with a friend, suppose that friend meets an acquaintance who is unknown to Alma, and stops to speak, should Alma stand also, or should she walk on? Or should Alma have a bowing acquaintance with her companion's friend, what should she do in that case, particularly if both companion and acquaintance are gentlemen? (In neither case should you leave your friend, who will introduce you, and you will merely bow.)

GIRL'S OWN PAPER, OCTOBER 3RD, 1885

Sack. How comes it that you sometimes walk with a gentleman, if not engaged to him? If your intended husband, you may, of course, walk under one umbrella; but otherwise you had better keep your own to yourself.

HOME COMPANION, 1885

The mere act of riding a bicycle is not in itself sinful 'Cyclos' (Rotherham), and if it is the only available means of reaching the church on Sunday it may be excusable. On the other hand, if walking or riding in the usual way is discarded for the sake of the exercise or exhilaration bicycle riding affords, it is clearly wrong. Besides, dignity of action and a noble decorum should be inseparable from the high office of Sunday-school teacher, and anything that impairs the dignity of that office necessarily impairs the influence as well. Bear this well in mind, 'Cyclos'.

John (Wolverhampton) is not a great traveller, but he is in quest of something which is far more precious than rubies. He wants a good wife and a good home. I am glad to hear it. If *John* will find the first, he will be sure to get the second. A good wife is worth far more than a gold-mine; but she is much easier to find, although *John* does not think so. He has been on this quest for the last twelve months, and now he tells me, in the most despairing manner, that he is afraid he will never find her. Do not give up hope, *John*. Go to some church or chapel, take an active share in the work of doing good, and you will soon become associated with young women who are fitted to make you a desirable helpmeet. 'The woman that feareth the Lord, she shall be praised.' And that is the woman you want. So try again, *John*.

MOTHERS AND DAUGHTERS, MAY, 1893

A sister. Make your brother happy at home and he will not want to spend his evenings away. Certainly sing him lively songs. Perpetual hymn-singing (if he cannot appreciate it) will not win him to love what is dearest to you. Let him feel your great desire is to please and study him, that the Christly principle of love rules your conduct. Opportunities will not be wanting in which you may sing more thoughtful songs, winning him to care for them because you do.

THE YOUNG WOMAN, 1893

. . . Given a desirable man among your acquaintances, I think you might not be afraid – but this is a great secret – to let him see, in a modest way, that you think well of him.

. . . That parents should prefer their daughters to marry into comfortable pecuniary circumstances is not altogether to be wondered at. . . . To marry on a very narrow income is to invite discomfort, which only a very strong and mutual affection would render tolerable.

MOTHERS AND DAUGHTERS, MAY, 1893

Pansy. No. Home-made wines are forbidden to the whole-hearted Total Abstainer. I am surprised you still use stimulants in cooking. It is cruel for your tempted servant. Many a poor cook has learnt to love strong drink in temperance households where wines and spirits have been used for flavouring.

OUR MOTHERS AND DAUGHTERS, 1893

James P. I am sorry for you, but a magazine intended for women readers, very specially, cannot be expected to put on record the ·case you deplore. Clearly you have been greatly to blame. You own to flirting, yet despise the girl who flirts with you – you thought her sincere. Why should she be more sincere than you are? I am honestly glad you have been entrapped in your own net, although I pity the girl who, clearly, by your example and influence has been false to all the noble instincts of true-hearted womanhood.

MOTHERS AND DAUGHTERS, JUNE, 1893

Annie P. I am so sorry for you. In your case it is undoubtedly true, 'It is better to have loved and lost, than never to have loved at all.' Contact with all who are definitely Christian is sure to be ennobling. On the other hand, friendship with the aimless and frivolous cannot be helpful. If being 'country cousin' means being simple and thoughtful for others, careful about personal expenditure, and glad to work in a Sunday school – the name is in itself a Degree.

HOME COMPANION, JANUARY, 1894

James H. In choosing your friends remember your mother and sister. Do not form a friendship with anyone whom you would hesitate to invite to your home. Your argument that a girl may be infinitely superior to the social position which her friends occupy may be quite true, but you must never lose sight of the fact that *marriage* will bring you in contact and close relationship with those whose tastes and habits are not at all likely to find kinship with your own. Why run these terrible risks? In justice to everybody concerned, be discreet.

I should not like to lay a heavy burden on your innocent seventeen-year-old conscience, so I will merely say that it is unfortunate that young girls get into the habit of meeting 'gentlemen' out walking; and that love-making under such circumstances is vulgar as well as unfortunate. The young man's theory that as long as you please yourselves it does not matter what people say, is probably only foolish in his case; in any case it has no value. Most stories of misfortune begin just as you describe, and therefore it might be well to drop the gentleman's acquaintance.

GIRL'S OWN PAPER, JANUARY 5TH, 1894

Melanie. According to present generally recognised custom there is no reason why you should not play cricket with your brothers or gentlemen friends, if you have a lady-friend with you, at least looking on. It is better not to call young men by their Christian names unless you have been well acquainted with each other from childhood.

GIRL'S OWN PAPER, OCTOBER 6TH, 1894

Tootsie. Go by all means to see your betrothed husband, but take your sister with you.

MOTHERS AND DAUGHTERS, NOVEMBER, 1894

I should certainly advise gentle but dignified resistance to the caresses you speak of, while the one to bestow them claims no greater position than that of friend. If caring for you in the noblest way (as he doubtless does) he will appreciate your objection and probably 'speak out' and thus remove it.

GIRL'S OWN PAPER, MARCH 2ND, 1895

Ta-ra-ra. It surprises us to find that a girl sufficiently educated to write and spell well should be so deplorably ignorant of the common rules of society to think she may go out alone with a young man in his canoe. And, furthermore, one whom she 'only knows slightly'.

Perplexed. I think it is the manner of dancing, not the physical exercise itself, that has caused the dance to fall into disrepute with many. I do not think round dances should ever have been introduced among refined nations. Many people protest, and I have no doubt with truth, that they see nothing objectionable in frisking round a room to the sound of music in the embrace of indiscriminate persons of the opposite sex, but others think it very ugly and in bad taste. . . . If the old fashioned dances, in which the partners stood apart and really danced, were introduced in influential circles, dancing parties would probably become as popular as they ever were. . . . To see children or girls of the lower classes dancing in the street to the sound of a barrel organ is to realise that the music and the motion both afford in themselves quite harmless pleasures, which have been spoiled, like many another pleasure, by grafting on them vulgar and extravagant excess.

HOME COMPANION, MARCH, 1896

G.Y.P. Do not lose heart. Alas! That doctors should, in spite of all their up to date experience, order stimulants to women as a medicine! Your sudden flight from total abstinence to insobriety is indeed terrible to contemplate. But as I think of your special case, two things strike me. Firstly, your own sorrow and your open confession of the fascinating power the drink is getting over you. Secondly, God's goodness and mercy and power to save. Claim His Power! Christ is the same yesterday, today and for ever! He will never cast out any who come to Him. He is able to save to the uttermost.

WOMAN'S LIFE, MARCH 14TH, 1896

Maggie's lover is always reading. That is, whenever he is in a train, a 'bus, or a tramcar with her, he takes out a book or paper and begins to devour the contents. Do I not think it rude, or, at any rate, forgetful?

Well, it all depends upon the surrounding circumstances. You know it is frequently most worrying to lovers, in either of the conveyances you mention, to talk when the afore-mentioned train, 'bus or tramcar is full of people. Maggie must remember that the man who loves a book is generally the man who stays at home; and when she is married, possibly she will not be sorry that her beau is a bit 'bookish'. It means an armchair, slippers, and fireside. Do you see what I mean, Maggie?

Harold, who writes from St. Albans – you see, even young men read my little Courtship Page! – is much distressed. His sweetheart, Madge, whom he declares to be very pretty, and to sing like an angel, has been reading a great deal about kissing being infectious, and it is with very great difficulty she will permit him to enjoy this privilege, which belongs to all good and true sweethearts. Harold wants to know if this is a sufficient reason for discontinuing their engagement?

Of course you won't discontinue your engagement. Show Madge this paragraph, and immediately proceed to kiss and make it up.

Puzzled asks right away: Please can you help me? My mother has gone into the country, and since she has been away a young man has often called on me and asked me to go out bicycle riding with him; should I accept in my mother's absence without her knowledge?

Evidently this young man is a friend of your family, or I presume he would not call so frequently upon you. This being the case, I really see no reason why you should not go out for an occasional ride with him. I think, however, so as to be perfectly straightforward in the matter, that when you write to your mother you could tell her that you have been out for an enjoyable little ride with this young gentleman.

A Lover who is a member of the sterner sex, has been keeping company with a young lady for about two years, and they both love one another very dearly. A short time ago he took her photograph to a phrenologist, who told him that they ought by no means to get married, as they were not suited to each other. My correspondent is greatly upset about this; has not told his sweetheart anything about it, and asks me what he should do.

Take no notice of what the phrenologist said; it it utter nonsense to suppose that anybody can possibly tell from a photograph what you were informed. I hope you will go on loving one another and be perfectly happy.

HOME COMPANION, AUGUST 7TH, 1897

F.P. No, I do not approve of plaid and coloured-striped stockings for bicycling. I think them vulgar in the extreme. They should be of the same colour of the shoes, black, white or brown.

HOME COMPANION, SEPTEMBER 3RD, 1898

'From the Old Armchair'

The only way to be beautiful, *Esmerelda,* is to be noble. If you are noble and good, you need not think that hard work will spoil your appearance. A young lady who has remarkably beautiful arms says she made them so by systematically exercising herself by sweeping carpets with a broom.

1900–1939

THE romantic atmosphere of Edwardian England broke down the terrified prudery, although basic etiquette remained decorous. But with the First World War even that went – formal introductions became superfluous when women were thrust into close working contact with all kinds and classes of men. At long last, after so many years of agitation, women were able to prove that they were not just wilting, domestic ornaments. In the joyous outburst after the war they took care there would be no retrenching by adopting masculine sportiness in clothes and manners. Aunt Aggies, naturally, didn't approve the new, abandoned mood, but gradually eased.

Do help me! writes Eugenie (Clapham Common). I am in great trouble. I am very much in love with a man who is in a lower position socially than myself. He is sweet and good, and is earning a sufficient salary to keep a wife in comfort. My friends say that if I marry him our married life will not be a happy one and they advise me to give him up; but we love each other so well that I cannot do this, and so write to you for advice.

If you are sure, Eugenie, that your love for this man is real and lasting, I do not think you will hesitate a moment considering his position. Ask yourself if you love him sufficiently to overlook his position; and if you do then by all means marry him and I sincerely hope that your married life will be a truly happy one.

THE COSY CORNER, 1905

Cupid's Cosy Corner

You are a very silly girl, *Loveless and Lonely,* to say you are in love with a man who was kind enough to help you find your way home in a fog. The very fact that he has taken no notice of you in the street since shows that his action had no higher meaning than a desire to help you out of a difficulty. You must not take the initiative and try to cultivate the acquaintance. I quite realise how difficult it is for a working-girl living in lodgings to make new friends, but, at the same time, you should remember that sooner or later Cupid comes to all; therefore your chance will come without you trying to force a love affair for yourself.

THE COSY CORNER, 1905

Your lover is very unsatisfactory, *E.D.* He has no business to court you for three years without saying anything definite, and you certainly should not encourage him to continue attentions that may mean nothing in the end. You say he is affectionate when you are alone, but often goes several weeks without attempting to see you. This does not look as if he cared much. Have you no father or brother who could ask him what he means?

I do not think your lover will give you up because you are so shy, *Constant Reader*. But can't you try and be a little more confiding with him? You say you are never happy out of his presence, yet you can't kiss him and tell him so. I believe you would find it quite easy to overcome your shyness if you would think a little less of yourself and a little more of Jim. Think what unutterable pleasure it would give him, if you put your arms round his neck and kissed him of your own free will! Don't be afraid to tell him that you love him; there is nothing to be ashamed of, and your shyness is robbing your engagement of half its sweetness. . . .

FAMILY FRIEND, 1906

Over the Teacups

Julia. You say you only went once into that doubtful company and don't intend to do it again. I sincerely hope you will not. Oh, I do earnestly entreat all young people who may read these lines to guard themselves against the first inroads into purity and high moral tone! Over and over again have I seen lives shipwrecked – all that is worth living for a woman lost – by tiny beginnings. A doubtful riddle, a jest with a low double meaning, an impure book, have ended for many a girl in being an outcast in society. You know very well what I mean. I will say no more. Only remember – nothing, nothing, can restore to a woman that sweet bloom of purity which is the crown God gave her.

Aunt Flo.

Nettie rather takes one's breath away by the frankness with which she states her trouble. 'He kisses and hugs me,' she says, 'and when he holds me to his bosom he calls it rapture. But I can't say that I do, for all the time my nose is on his neck I am thinking of the pomade he uses on his hair, and the horrid starchiness of his collar – it sometimes scratches so. And when we are out for walks (I rather like the walks, being in the house all day) he gushes about the moon, and calls me names – "fair Luna" and such-like – and quotes poetry about the stars, and says something to the effect that I'm another. He speaks of "thrills", and "rapture", and "bliss", and things of that sort I feel nothing about. The only thing I am sure of is this – that mother says he is the best man I ever shall get, and I must take care not to vex him.'

Here is simplicity! Here is guilelessness! And it is all so intensified when she comes to the point – 'Can you tell me, dear editor, what love really is?' I have my own idea, of course, but it isn't this way. I think it is two helping one another, as two chums might be in the same business – each working for the other, and each fairly sharing in the profits.

I'm afraid I can't – to 'Nettie'. That line about 'my nose on his neck' has quite reduced all my ideas to pulp. . . . I fear I can only give 'Nettie' the old, old definition that love is 'an itching at the heart one can't get scratching'. If she doesn't feel that, then the best thing she can do is to look out for some man of the same mind as herself, marry him, and become a good book-keeper to him. Two people will then be satisfied – with themselves at least.

COSY CORNER, OCTOBER 6TH, 1906

My sweetheart tells me that it is quite the thing now for women to smoke cigarettes, and that all nice girls smoke. Would you learn to do so, if you were I, asks Isobel.

Certainly not, *Isobel*, although there is nothing vulgar in itself in women smoking; yet there is still so much prejudice against it that it is only quite the most go-ahead girls who would smoke in the presence of a gentleman. You have existed so far without this craving, so there is no need for you to go in for it at your sweetheart's suggestion. I have heard of wives smoking to keep their husbands company, but I do not think a sweetheart should be so far indulged.

Ethel. If your fiancé goes to no place of worship on Sunday, and you find from his conversation that religion has no place in his life's programme, then beware! I do not say you should give him up, but on no account marry him until you see a change. Why should not *you* help to make him different! Oh! We women little realise what influence for good we can wield in a man's life. Men have to leave the home nest very early, and they face the temptations and snares of the world often but ill-prepared. And we women could often step in and be the Lord's handmaids in presenting to them all that is beautiful and good in life, and we *don't*. Ah! we should have a great deal to answer for, we women. . . . Think over what I have said. You will soon see if your influence is really having a permanent effect on your fiancé's character and habits. If not —, don't marry him.

COSY CORNER, JULY 7TH, 1906

Halma is one of three girls who are going on the moors for their holidays. Our sweethearts want to come with us, she says. Would it be right for them to stay in the same house with us? We think, perhaps, they would not like to stay amongst strangers.

Possibly not, *Halma.* But surely they would like even less to do anything that might in any way compromise you. There is no reason why they should not spend their holidays in the neighbourhood where you are going, and they can, of course, see you frequently and arrange to have all sorts of delightful excursions in your company. But I do not think they ought to stay in the same house with you. Your good name is too precious a thing for you to risk even the slightest breath of suspicion against it.

Typist. I do not think you are quite fair to your employer in complaining of your isolated position in his office; you knew how it would be before you accepted the situation, and it is yourself or your parents who must be responsible for this. You surely could not expect he would employ you, and also a chaperone to look after you! It is one of the inevitable changes which must be faced when young women go out to business – that they must be self-reliant, and trust to God and themselves for their safeguarding, just as with every lad. These attentions which your employer's son has been paying you may mean much – and an ugly 'much' – or they may mean only the outcome of a good-natured disposition. . . . It seems to me quite clear that somehow you must refuse these gifts, or you may soon find them the pioneers to requests for favours which you will then have more difficulty in declining, possibly to your subsequent sorrow. . . .

THE GIRL'S COMPANION, 1908

Two Young Girls ask: Is there any harm in a young lady permitting a gentleman whom she met at the seashore, and to whom she has not been formally introduced, to see her home?

My dears, there are few graver follies committed by the thoughtless and heedless than forming the acquaintance of strangers in the way you describe.

Unfortunately, men are not labelled, informing the world at large, women in particular, of their calling.

The handsome, debonair, well-dressed, agreeable young man may be the daring thief who broke into your house last year; or the highwayman who held up your next door neighbour only the month before, leaving him for dead on the pavement from a blow from a concealed murderous pair of brass knuckles which he usually carries with him.

Or he may be an escaped madman who has just broken his way out of some insane asylum.

Such people have a peculiar mania for making the acquaintance of young girls wherever they come across them, and talk and behave so rationally that their real condition is not discovered until some terrible deed has been accomplished by them.

The girl who will flirt with and talk to a stranger, honourable young men shun if they are looking for a wife. Remember that.

I wonder if you will think me very wicked when I tell you that though I am a married woman, I do not love my husband and am not living with him? We married too young – I was eighteen and he twenty – and I soon discovered that he was not the man for me. Soon after I met the one man for me and though we have never been sweethearts, yet we have confessed our love. . . . Is it my duty to live with a man I do not love, when all my heart belongs to another?. . . Do you think I am acting wickedly and ought I to go back to the man I married?

Hester.

Not wicked, *Hester,* but foolish and weak, dear. We cannot break away from sacred promises. When you took that man for your husband you undertook certain duties, that you are morally bound to fulfil – to help him, to comfort him, to cherish him, to make a home for him, to lead him towards a better land. Your married life has disappointed you. Well, often things we buy turn out quite different from what we hope they will but we cannot cast them away and have our money back. . . . Return to your husband, bury the love that can be nothing to you, and determine if you cannot care for him as a wife should, to do your duty. . . .

My boy has been in the trenches for six months and expects to get furlough any moment. What I want to ask is this: if you were me would you meet him at the station or would you wait for him at home?

You ask me a difficult question, little girl, and I find it very hard to advise you. Were I you I'd want with all my heart and soul to be the first woman my boy would see when he arrived. And yet, dear, meeting him after all he has gone through would mean so much to me and to him that I don't think I could bear to see him in public.

Really and truly, were I you, I'd wait for him alone some-where – at home if possible. Somehow, such a meeting is too sacred to be witnessed by anybody. But be there if you can to see him off when he leaves for the Front again, and be as brave as you can, dear.

You were quite right not to encourage the young man, Mabel. I know how lonely you are, dear, and for a lonely girl Sheffield is not the cheeriest of places, is it? But it's a big risk allowing a stranger to talk to you without an introduction.

Don't think I am prudish or narrow minded. I'm not, but I know how little men think of girls who, what they call, 'make themselves cheap'. And any girl who allows herself to be picked up does make herself cheap. Fight down the loneliness, and go home for the weekends as often as you can. There is nothing worth having that has not been fought for. Remember that, and if you struggle to keep yourself for Mr Somebody, Mr Somebody will come along before you know where you are. But you won't find him ogling in the streets, dear.

Our Family Club, conducted by Mother

Dear Mother. I have a sweetheart although I am only 18. Do you think I am too young to have one? I don't mean to get married for a few years as I am a great help to my parents; also mother isn't very strong, and I help all I can when I come home at night. Mother is the dearest and best of mothers. I wonder if you think I am doing wrong, for mother really doesn't know that I am keeping company with my young man? I am too shy to tell her, also I am sure she would think I am too young. Do you think I should stop going out with him until I am a little bit older? I like him better than anyone; and he does me, and talks to me of the future. Do tell me what you think I ought to do.

A Scottish Daughter.

Come, my dear member, you have the dearest and sweetest of mothers, and yet you are deceiving her. Oh, how it will pain her when she knows her little daughter is acting so! Tell her at once lassie, and get her consent to bring this gentleman home to be introduced to her. Eighteen is not too young to start 'courting' if you do it openly and your people approve. I never advise a secret engagement, because happiness never results from it. Yes, there is harm in 'keeping company' secretly. Dear daughter, put yourself in mother's place. If you had a daughter, how would you feel if she deceived you? Don't you remember saying these words:

> There's a wicked spirit
> Watching round you still
> And he tries to tempt you
> To all harm and ill.
>
> But you must not heed him,
> You must learn to fight
> With the bad within you
> And to do the right.

So to mother at once, dear daughter, own up to your deception. She won't scold you; she will only help you to choose aright.

THE HOME MIRROR, JUNE 19TH, 1920

Afraid. Get along with you! You're surely not afraid of boys. Why, we're not cannibals these days, and unlikely to eat you! Go about, mix with all sorts of boys and girls, and soon that frightened feeling will wear off, and confidence will be established. No doubt there is a boy somewhere who wants to meet you, but if you look at him as you say you do you'll frighten him in his turn. . . .

THE HOME MIRROR, JUNE 26TH, 1920

J.L.D. (Yorks). I can understand the point of view of this young man. There is no real harm in a girl smoking, but I am sure she adds nothing to her charms by indulging in it. To be sweet and womanly is what a girl should aim at being, and I am certain she will not make her task any the easier by puffing cigarettes. Still, I know it's not a sin. Men are queer things, aren't they?

POLLY'S PAPER, APRIL 18TH, 1921

Worried I.C. Personally, I can't bear to be kissed, and in any case I don't think it nice for boys and girls to kiss all round, as you seem to be doing. And yet everything depends on the way a kiss is given and received. Perhaps it would be as well if you told your friend you would rather her boy did not kiss you, and then after a time you could tell your boy not to kiss her. Only don't do it ill-temperedly, just in a light, pleasant way. . . .

POLLY'S PAPER, NOVEMBER 28TH, 1921

At a party the other night my girl friends and I had an argument over 'Are girls fast who use powder?' Perhaps you will tell us what you think?

My opinion is that it's a question of fashion and nothing else. Hundreds of nice girls use powder, and so do thousands of girls who are not nice, so people are apt to mistake the one for the other.

Polly's Unknown Friend. You have given me a sleepless night. I am so anxious over your letter. I am a woman of the world, my dear. I am not a bit straight-laced, indeed I shock some people by my views, but with all my soul I beg you not to listen to the temptation. . . .

GIRL'S COMPANION, NOVEMBER 19TH, 1921

Cassie J. writes to ask if it is right to kiss a boy before you are engaged to him. She has been walking out with her boy for six months, but they not engaged, nor even thinking about it.

There is not much harm in a 'good night kiss', Cassie, but personally, I do not think it right to be always kissing. Friendship with a boy can be as sincere without kissing, and often the kisses are only 'swank', you know.

HOME MIRROR, SEPTEMBER 9TH, 1922

Alice R. Don't be silly! Accept this boy's invitation, and learn to play tennis. Don't be afraid to start; too many girls are like that, and consequently, in the end, learn to do nothing at all. The popular girl is the girl who can turn her hand to anything; and if she can play games, all the better for the boys!

HOME MIRROR, NOVEMBER 18TH, 1922

B.G. (Sutton). Old lad, she's shy, that's all. Just shy and can't pluck up courage to say what she wants to say and be natural. It is so rare – and so refreshing nowadays – to come across a really shy lass, that I should say you will be lucky if you win her for your sweetheart, for shy girls are usually nice girls. Why not say one night: 'See here, Polly (or whatever her name may be), I've bought two nice seats for the music-hall and you are coming along with me.' Take the bull by the horns, as they say, B.G. That's the way with shy lassies.

Pegs. At sixteen it is charming to be shy, horrid to be pert and forward, so don't try to make yourself any different from what you are now, girlie. Blushes on the cheek of sweet sixteen are quite adorable and I wouldn't help you to stop blushing, my dear, even if I could. Don't be in a hurry getting to know 'boys'. There's lots of time for you to look round yet.

I am a factory girl and have been keeping company with a young man who is far above my own position. His people are tradespeople. We have been friendly now for over two years, but I do not think his parents knew until quite recently that he wanted me to become engaged to him and told them about me. They refuse to meet me and his mother wrote me a very cruel letter saying that I should ruin his life by marrying him and that she would never allow a factory girl as her daughter-in-law.

You are both old enough to know your own minds and you love one another. I think that is all that matters.

Tilly. It'll take a bit of explaining, won't it? When the boy you love saw you in the arms of another man, of course, there were ructions.

Why did you do it, dear? Wasn't it too utterly silly for words? Just for the sake of a little fun! It wasn't fun, but foolishness, *Tilly*. But it's taught you a lesson, and we can never learn too much.

The only course open to you is to confess the truth. That you were carried away and meant nothing by your action.

That all your love is for your own dear boy, and you're really and truly sorry. It's his love that'll forgive you, *Tilly,* and DON'T DO IT AGAIN! Love doesn't stand larking with.

Ethel. No, dear, it's not *your* place to make advances to him. If he has been looking and smiling at you in the same railway carriage every morning for the past three months, and if, as you say, he deliberately looks along the train to find where you are, then you may depend upon it that *very* shortly he will speak to you. Then I hope that you will find that he lives up to all that you believe him to be. He certainly seems a wonderful boy from your description, dear. I, too, think that there is always something so *clean* and attractive about a boy with fair, curly hair, clear complexion, and twinkling blue eyes.

Margery. My home is in Scotland and I am in business in London. I live alone in a bed-sitting room. For the last six months I have been courting a young man and last Sunday I invited him to tea. I did not think there was any harm in this until his mother told me she did not think it very wise.

I am inclined to agree with your boy's mother about his visiting you in your room. I am sure that, as far as you are both concerned, it was perfectly innocent, but, unfortunately, some folk are inclined to regard these things in a far from charitable light, and a girl cannot afford to risk her reputation. If you invite him again, try to get a friend or another couple to come along, too.

ANN TEMPLE'S HUMAN CASEBOOK

I have an elderly cousin, a very correct dowager, who insists that she should act as chaperone at the tea parties I give in my flat. She tells me a bachelor host must have an elderly woman as hostess. I feel sure this is an out-moded custom, but should be glad of reassurance from you. – Bachelor.

Not for tea parties! Modern bachelors give their own parties, even to pouring out the tea and recommending this or that cake, sandwich and cigarette. It is still considered correct for the chaperone to be present, guarding the proprieties at a formal luncheon or dinner party and at any function when only one women guest is invited.

WOMAN'S OWN, MAY 30TH, 1936

I suppose you will think me very old-fashioned, but I do want your advice. My daughter wants to go on a hiking holiday this year with a group of boys and girls, and I am rather worried about it. She is only seventeen, and I do not know what might happen. Do you think it is a good idea for a young girl to spend a whole fortnight in the company of young men?

I don't think you will have anything to worry about if your daughter goes with a group of young people. To begin with, if walking all day they will, most of them, feel like a good meal and then sleep. As well as that, young people are different now than they were in your day and most of them could go off on holidays in couples and be quite safe and happy. . . .

DAILY MAIL, JUNE 10TH, 1936

Now that the hot weather is here I notice that my girl employees are arriving in the offices in short sleeves. I have no personal prejudice against the practice but would like to know whether this is becoming a general practice. – A.C.

As long as the general effect is trim and workmanlike, I do not think short sleeves are taboo anywhere. The fashion certainly helps typists to remain cool, and one must not forget the economy effected, for long, light-coloured sleeves become quickly soiled.

A MODERN DAUGHTER

My daughter is just eighteen. She is very attractive and has lots of men friends, many of whom I have never met. I don't want to be Victorian, but I feel that it is not right for her to accept invitations from these men until I have approved of them. I don't know what to say, however, as all her girl friends are allowed to do exactly as they wish.   *Worried Mama.*

Of course you want to know the people your daughter is being friendly with. Why not ask her to bring new friends to tea or dinner at your house before she accepts invitations from them? I am sure she will appreciate that you only want to take care of her.

I suppose I am an old-fashioned type of woman, but I do find my new daughter-in-law's unconventional style of dressing very trying. She rarely wears a hat, and if she does it is only a minute cap hidden in her curls. I don't think this is a sufficiently dignified style for a young married woman. . . . W.A.

I can quite understand that you feel irritated by a style of dress that would have been termed undignified when you were married, but one simply must allow for a change in conventions. . . .

Mrs W.L. You and your husband are so happy and con-
tented in your love for each other, my dear, that I certainly do
not think you need listen to the warnings of those who say you
are allowing him too much freedom, just because you consent to
his staying the night at his sister's on 'club' nights, and thus
avoiding a long journey home. You know where he is, there is no
secrecy about it, you love and trust each other, and I think, therefore, you would be most unwise to make any alteration. As long
as there is such a good understanding between you and him,
you need fear nothing, little wife.

WOMAN'S WEEKLY, OCTOBER 2ND, 1937

I am 24 and feel that it is time I thought of marrying, but
tonight I told my young man that I could not marry him because
he will never raise his hat when we meet. He says that this proves
only that I do not love him. What do you think?

It seems to me very sad to quarrel over such a little thing. How
can you expect happiness when married if you quarrel so now?
I agree that it is an act of courtesy for a man to raise his hat when
he meets a lady but I do not think his failing to do this should
cause a quarrel. What I do think is serious is his unwillingness to
meet you over something you feel strongly about. Would a man
who will not do this little thing for you be likely to make a good
husband? . . .

D.W.B.E.—F

I am very anxious to get married some day and have a husband and children, but I don't really like men at all. What is the matter with me?

I wish you had told me your age. Most girls in their teens like feminine society better than masculine, but switch over to the opposite sex about the age of eighteen. Maybe you are later than some girls in doing so. Get about more, meet men, and see how you get on with them. If you find you really don't like them, go in for work with children, but don't marry just because you want to be a mother. . . .

WOMAN'S HOUR, APRIL 22ND, 1935

Our Friendship Page

Tell Your Troubles to Violet Crauford.

Bert in Doubt writes: Please will you help me with my problem? Five years ago when I was twenty I got a job in London and while I was there I had a love affair with a married woman. It only lasted three months, for then I lost my job and returned to my home up North where I have been working ever since. I have never bothered with girls until a few months ago, then I took up with a real nice girl and she has promised to marry me. Now, this is my trouble: I have never told her about that affair in London. Ought I to do so, do you think? I dread the thought of it as she is such a straight, innocent sort of girl, but I want to do what is fair and square.

Cheer up, Bert! For really, old man, I don't think there is any necessity to mention the affair to your sweetheart, since it happened long before you met her, and you are never likely to see the other woman again. Good luck! May every happiness be yours now that you have found the Right Girl.

WOMAN'S OWN, JUNE 15TH, 1935

Several of my boy friends have asked me to go out with them,
but I have never been able to accept this because I have heard that
a girl's life can be spoilt by this sort of thing. Is this true?

Not if a girl is sensible and knows what she is doing. Life would
be very grim if boys and girls could not associate together happily,
wouldn't it? If you will write to me privately, I will give you some
sound 'motherly' advice about life. . . .

WOMAN'S OWN, MARCH 21ST, 1936

I have been in love with Bertie for two years; once he put his
arms round me when helping me over a stile. I go about with a
lot of other men, but he doesn't mind. Do you think he cares
for me?

I think he just wants to be friendly. I wouldn't think about him
too seriously, if I were you. There is not much point in wondering
about a young man who does not really love you, is there? . . .

DAILY MAIL, MARCH 6TH, 1937

My daughter, aged twenty, and a man friend, aged twenty-six,
to whom she will probably become engaged, want to go away for
their summer holidays together. They propose going to a holiday
camp. I do not know whether to allow it or not. I certainly would
not have been allowed to do it before I married. But I recognise
that custom has changed.

It is a growing custom for young people to take their holidays
in friendly groups, staying all together and making up parties for
their sports and outings. They count the 'group' sufficient
chaperonage. I doubt whether it is wise for two young people to
join a camp where they know no-one else; where they do
not join with the joint activities. I expect I shall be thoroughly
old-fashioned, but I maintain that there is a great strain on
the pre-engagement relationship in having exclusive holiday
companions.

73

I have been friendly with a boy for two years and I am very fond of him. He says if I really loved him I would give myself to him. I don't want to lose him, but I don't feel it is right.

Don't let him persuade you. Some boys seem to think there is nothing in courtship but one physical fact. Some things can wait until after marriage, my dear, and courtship is a time when you should find out about each other's interests, hopes and fears, loves and hates. It is still true that a man might take an 'easy' girl around, but that is not the kind he marries or wants to provide for.

WOMAN'S OWN, MARCH 5TH, 1938

My son likes smart people and smart things and now he is going to marry a girl whom I can only call modern. I cannot believe he can be happy with quite so sophisticated and undomesticated a girl and would do anything to break things off.

Your son is the one doing the marrying, you know! Leave him to choose the girl he wants. Actually, you are mistaken about these modern girls. Under that hard veneer they are as soft and sentimental as the rest of us and as good housewives. Owing to their business training, they often make less of a mess of things than we did when we first married. . . .

'Ann Hirst Advises'

I have been engaged to him for three years. He has had three different cars in the time we've been going about together. My people asked him some time ago when he intended to get married. He said just as soon as he got his car paid for. Now he has changed his car again – for a new one this time – and has said nothing about marriage.

Decidedly, you should find out if or when this young man intends to marry. If he is still indefinite and has some excuse such as he gave before I think you should consider yourself unengaged and free to go out with other men.

DAILY MAIL, JUNE 5TH, 1939

There is a scarcity of good maids in this district and we are frequently without any. At such a time should not a husband help by at least cleaning his own shoes? I can do every other menial and laborious task with perfect good humour but as his wife just cannot bear having to clean his shoes. – P.

But when you come to think of it, shoe cleaning is only part of the usual household routine. Back in your mind somewhere is an idea that it is a mark of servitude – linked up with the ceremony of obeisance.

It is not really the job that irritates you; it is a secret grudge against having to play the part of a drudge, a little private quarrel with your own personality which you ought to settle for once and for all.

75

1940 onwards

WHERE the tensions of the First World War sent men and women flirting, the Second World War sent them into even closer contact and there are an increasing number of queries about sex before marriage. After the war the whole subject of sex – both inside and outside marriage – became more outspoken and Aunt Aggies, with their matter-of-fact advice, are largely responsible for today's level-headed attitudes.

Aunt Aggies have increased in importance, too, as the influence of Church, school and parents has declined. Their combined mail must be in the region of 1,500 letters a week, each one representing an agonising personal problem. John Dunton's original idea has turned into a vast welfare service, a corporate mother, father, psychiatrist and priest that now has more influence than any other body in guiding the nation's morals.

I am trying to be patriotic and am wearing last winter's coat, but my boy friend keeps criticising and saying war savings are all wrong. This makes me very unhappy and I wonder whether to get engaged on my next birthday or not.

The fact that you are patriotic and saving and he is not shows how differently you look at life; and your feeling of doubt shows that you are not happy. I would give him up – two such different people, one with ideals and one without, would never get on.

WOMAN'S OWN, MARCH 22ND, 1941

I feel very worried about my husband. We used to be so happy, but since the "Blitz" he never seems to want to kiss or make love to me when we are at home. Do you think there is someone else?

No. What I think is that all the nervous stress of your present mode of life is preying on his mind and nerves. . . . Make him comfortable, cheer him up, but don't expect any love-making. Many women have the same experience at present, and it is all part of the war, nothing personal.

WOMAN'S OWN, JANUARY 23RD, 1942

I am serving in the Forces and find I am going to have a baby. Two men could be responsible, but I don't know which. Both have offered to marry me, but I can't decide which. Would it be better to throw them both over and make a fresh start?

Much better. You don't love either of them and whoever marries you will never feel sure of you. Get over this trouble, make up your mind to be morally stronger in the future, and marry when you find a man you can really love; moreover, a man who will respect you before marriage.

EVELYN HOME

My husband is being invalided home from abroad. He has been away now nearly four years. At first when I received the news I was wildly happy, but as the time approaches I am getting more and more frightened. I know I have changed a lot through the war – I work in an office which I never did before, I live in a city and I used to live in deep country, I have learned to like theatres, cinemas, art galleries, restaurants and shops. On the other hand I know from my husband's letters that all he wants is to come back to everything exactly as it was. Of course, I may love it but I'm terrified I shan't like him as a husband again.

If you have changed, I'm sure you will find your husband has too. He will have become more tolerant, broader-minded, quicker to understand your altered attitude. . . . As to the marriage relationship, I think that you will find if your husband is still loving and considerate, he will be patient and gentle with you and help you to re-adapt yourself to the old happy partnership.

WOMAN, APRIL 27TH, 1946

My husband has returned home after three years in a Japanese prison camp. I thought we should be able to carry on where we left off – but I now find myself repelled by him.

We have been married nine years and have two children. I have always been faithful to him, lived for the day when he would return and am still very much in love with him. Yet I somehow cannot return the affection he still feels for me.

The first thing to do is to tell your husband you are as much in love with him as ever – then tell him the rest of the story. In all probability you are suffering from a reaction now that the days of bitter anxiety and worry are over – you are exhausted emotionally. . . . Go to your doctor for a tonic and try to have a rest from home cares as much as possible. Don't pick up the threads where you left them – start all over again, as man and girl. . . .

HELEN GRAY

How can you tell if you are in love? I have been going out with a very nice boy. I think about him a lot, I feel I'd like to get married to him, but when he kisses me I don't get any thrill and haven't any feeling of wild happiness.

There's no real thermometer for testing love and even if there were I think that quite often emotions which were only 'warm' would last out 'boiling hot' or 'tropical' loves!

HOME COMPANION, APRIL 7TH, 1951

RUBY M. AYRES

My Ellen has always been a good daughter, but now she has taken up with a man her father and I couldn't possibly consent to her marrying. I'm not being snobbish, but he really doesn't belong to her class. Ellen went to school until she was eighteen and she's got a very good job as a secretary in a shipping office. She's twenty-three now and has never wanted for boy-friends of the right type – boys who share her interests, like going to the ballet and playing tennis. But she is completely infatuated with this Bill, who is no more than a labourer and whose interests are football, the pictures and dancing. She met him at a public dance hall and he has taken her to football matches and once even to 'the dogs'. . . . If she marries him her whole life will be ruined. . . .

With all sympathy for you, I think you are making a mistake to object to this man merely because he is not quite the class you would like your daughter to marry into. You may be shocked to know that I go to 'the dogs' myself and thoroughly enjoy it. Things are very different now from what they were in the days when you and I were young. If Ellen really loves this man, I can see no reason why they should not be happy together. He may make her a very good husband. . . .

*My friend and I are both in our teens, and work in an office
with two men. One of them says frankly that he uses talcum
powder and a deodorant and we are disgusted with this. Surely
he can't be manly? . . .*

. . . Most men need deodorants and talcum even more than
women, especially at this time of the year, when the far heavier
clothes of a man make personal freshness even more difficult
for him. . . .

*I have been married for twenty-eight years to a very good
husband, and have had four children who were my whole life, but
are all now married. My husband and I live alone in our comfortable modern home and we are completely bored. We never go out,
do nothing, and show each other no affection as we are middle-
aged. It is just washing, cooking and housework, day after day,
for me.*

Perhaps the demands of your family when young made you
push your love for your husband into the background. . . . Try to
talk to him as openly as you did in the early days of your marriage. Tell him how lost you feel, and I'm sure he will gladly
realize how dependent you are on his love. Then try together to
re-discover the interests and hobbies you shared before the
babies came. . . .

MARJORIE PROOPS

My husband faithfully promised to buy me a fur stole for my birthday. Now he says I can have a handbag instead as fur, he says, won't suit me. What do you think of a man who breaks a promise like this?

He's a skunk.

What can I do with my old man who will persist in calling me 'Ducks'?

Quack.

My friend says she will never get married but will take a lover as marriage means nothing nowadays. What are your views?

Your friend needs to have her head examined. Tell her it's time she grew up.

Dear Marje, I am 26 years old and have been going out with a 30-year-old man for three years. In that time he has proposed to me twice, but nothing has ever come of it. What is your advice?
Waiting.

What was it he proposed?

Dear Marje, I am very worried about my 17-year-old daughter. She has been going steady with her boy-friend for over a year. He is 20. Recently I found out that they are having sexual intercourse quite often. I hinted to her that I knew and she just looked ashamed and didn't say anything. I have always been frank with her so that she knows everything and I have always trusted her. What am I to do now?
Upset.

Short of locking her up every night, you cannot stop her from having intercourse with her boy friend. If you play the heavy mother and forbid her to see him, she will probably meet him secretly, and you will have built a barrier between you instead of a bridge. You must try to get her to talk to you about it so that you can at least make sure she is taking adequate birth control measures. If you tackle her sympathetically without criticism, she may confide in you and you will be able to help her make the right decision. If you just let things slide in the hope that everything will be all right in the end – well, both you and your daughter may suffer.

'The Informer'

From 'James the First', Earls Court, London

To put it simply, how do you get rid of a bird?

There are ways. You can post her on to me, for one thing. But a recent article in the American *Life* magazine quoted TV mogul James Aubrey Jnr. as advising a man to do it over a very good lunch.

He suggests it is much easier in the daytime – as there is more general optimism about while it is light. 'Buy her a big drink,' he says, 'and then tell her the train has reached Chicago and you're getting off at Chicago.'

Tell her she deserves a family life and you, you rotter, aren't the marrying kind. Then buy her a big lunch and let her absorb the news while she is eating. . . . Apparently this doesn't fail in America.

I doubt its efficiency here. Most of our British women are tenacious enough to swallow the food and then start arguing.

There is really only one way to get rid of a girl – and you have to be prepared to make her glad to be rid of you.

Just cultivate a few disgusting habits. This is foolproof but hardly ever used – simply because the average man wants a woman to stop bothering him, but he cannot stand the idea of her stopping adoring him.

MIRABELLE, MARCH 25TH, 1967

We are fourteen. Every time we get a date we don't turn up. The other day we arranged to meet two boys. When we saw them waiting for us, we were so embarrassed we ran away! What on earth can we do?   *Lesley and Jacky, Hayes.*

Better stick with the group till your confidence increases . . . and your manners improve! Rude and childish behaviour of this kind can only mean you are not ready to date yet.

MIRABELLE, APRIL 1ST, 1967

I am the only girl in our group who still hasn't got a trouser suit and I feel odd without one. All that holds me back is worrying I might look even more odd with one – I've got rather big hips.   *Jenny, Oxford.*

Invest in a good pantie girdle. Then go and try on some well cut suits. Take with you your most brutally frank friend! In a not too bold design, you should rate a pass.

MIRABELLE, MAY 20TH, 1967

My father's ever so strict about my boy friends. I don't know what he'll say about Tony – his hair's shoulder length. I can't avoid taking him home much longer.   *Vanessa, Tilbury.*

Is Tony a football star, kind to his granny? Mention it to Dad (casually, so he doesn't scent a snag!) and wedge news of his hairstyle somewhere among the virtues! Create a favourable impression early, and chances are Dad'll reserve judgement till he and Tony can really get acquainted.

MIRABELLE, MAY 27TH, 1967

I'm thrilled! I've just discovered a boy I like is writing my name all over his books. He's told people he wants to ask me out. But how long will I have to wait before he does?   *Norma, Falmouth.*

Just till he works up the nerve! Let him feel you are interested by acting pleasant and friendly. Should be all the encouragement he needs!

I would like to go out with a coloured boy I have met at work. I have known him for eight months, and have grown to like him very much, and I know he is fond of me. My parents have seen him, and they said he was all right, but when I told them I wanted to go out with him they objected. I am twenty years old and not a flighty type. I love my parents and don't like to disobey them, but I feel I must not give way to them on this matter.

It is only in the last ten years or so that we have had so many coloured people in this country, and compared with our reader, people of her parents' generation probably find it very difficult to feel at ease with people of a different colour. Their daughter has grown up with children of various races, and can assess this young man by his real value. Obviously she thinks him worthwhile, or she would not wish to go out with him. But while her parents may like him, they would be reluctant to accept him as a future son-in-law. Their fear is a real one, for they know that a marriage between different races has to face many extra difficulties because of dissimilar family customs and traditions. At twenty, our reader must be allowed to choose her own friends, but for the boy's sake as well as her own, she should not allow his friendship to develop without a great deal of careful thought.

Mum was thrilled when I mentioned a boy had asked me to go to a dance with him. She rushed out and bought me a new dress. The thing is, I am only twelve, I don't particularly like the boy and I'm not keen at the idea of going at all.   Carol, Ilford.

Then don't! As long as you rave over the dress and get plenty of wear out of it, your mother won't be too disappointed. Don't kick yourself afterwards for missing your dance, though!

My boy is crazy about Cilla Black – and I know I look a bit like her. Do you think he's going out with me just because of this?
Jill, Egham.

No, Jill. Obviously he likes the Cilla Black type – and you are like enough to be just that. Boys fall for one special girl for many reasons, and I am sure he likes you for yourself, otherwise he would not be dating you. What attracted you to him, anyway?

WOMAN'S REALM, DECEMBER 23RD, 1967

CLARE SHEPHERD

My 17-year-old daughter has become pregnant. When I talked about it to her and the boy who is responsible, they both said they did not wish to marry, partly for financial reasons and partly because they did not think they were ready for marriage. They say they will have the baby adopted. I do not believe in forced marriages, but it seems that they just wish to carry on as if nothing had happened. She still brings the boy home frequently and they do not seem to realise the seriousness of what they have done. I am appalled by the way they behave. What do you think I should do?

I agree with you that this young couple are showing a total disregard for your very natural feelings of dismay and worry. However, I do not think you should cut your daughter off from the support and affection of the father of her child, for it is better that he should be with her and not desert her, as so many young men do in this situation. So do not try to prevent them from meeting. If the boy is prepared to allow her to go through the pain of a child only to lose it unnecessarily in the end, your daughter will eventually realise that he is a useless person as far as she is concerned. But it may be that this couple are genuinely fond of one another and just have no inkling of the feelings of love and responsibility that the baby will arouse in them when it eventually arrives.

Index